LEAN
LABOR

A Survival Guide For Companies Facing Global Competition

GREGG GORDON

This book is dedicated to the people who make the products that improve our lives.

Written by: Gregg Gordon

ISBN: (13 digit) 978-0-615-44390-4

This book was printed in China by:

ONE WORLD PRESS

890 Staley Lane

Chino Valley, AZ 86323

800-250-8171

www.oneworldpress.com

on behalf of Kronos Publishing

a division of

Kronos Incorporated

297 Billerica Rd.

Chelmsford, MA 01730

+1 (978) 250-9800

Book and cover design: Nic Valentino

TABLE OF CONTENTS

Acknowledgements

Michele Glorie had the vision to suggest a book on this topic almost three years ago and rallied the many people required to make it a reality. Her support throughout the process is appreciated.

Indrani Ray-Ghosal managed the publishing process, made sure all the resources required were available, and kept me focused. Preston Gralla, who edited the book, was critical in teaching me the basics of authoring a book as well as improving it through his own efforts. Nic Valentino provided the cover design and graphics. Bala Zuccarello from One World Publishing provided guidance to ensure printing and distribution went smoothly. Additional help to create the book was also provided by Kylene Batsford, Tom Pappalardo, Lisa Pratt and Nandini Sen.

Charlie Dewitt began collaborating on the ideas in this book five years ago when we sat down and applied supply chain principles to workforce processes. His contributions didn't stop there. Charlie's coaching and suggestions left the book significantly better than the first draft he read.

Every example in this book has been put into practice by manufacturers, which means many people need credit for sharing their experiences. My colleagues include Joe Scheller, Peter Brabenec, Beth Berndt, Matt Hoak, Simon MacPherson and Gil Sullivan.

There were also several important contributors to the book who continue to practice Lean on a daily basis. Mark Nguyen, Michel Boeckx, Michele Cyrus, John Russo, Jason Fenske, Phil Hobel, Jenine Bogrand and Jeff Dart have all spent many years improving workforce practices at their companies and generously shared their stories and ideas with me.

Finally thanks to my family; Marnie, Travis, and Judy who encouraged me during the project and provided valuable feedback.

INTRODUCTION

I always look forward to watching "How It's Made" - a television show that goes on site to different manufacturers and films the production process. "How It's Made" has taken my favorite part of visiting a manufacturer, the production tour, and condensed it into a narrated, step-by-step 10 minute segment. The show documents a company's manufacturing process from issuing raw materials to packaging a finished product.

I wonder if the show's producers realize that in editing the actual video to fit into the show's time constraints, what they have really done for the manufacturer is provide a vision of perfect execution. During each segment, machines never break down, there's never a "cut to commercial" waiting for a critical operator to arrive, and material never warps ruining a production run. It's a production manager's dream, everything goes according to plan.

With "How It's Made" providing this vision of idealized production, is it possible for a manufacturer to transform its processes to achieve the perfect day, every day?

There's good reason to consider this; developed countries have been losing manufacturing jobs at an alarming rate over the past two decades to low-wage countries such as China and Mexico. Even China, with what many consider to be extremely low wage workers, is not immune to the impact of even lower-wage competition. A second generation of modern industrial workers is entering the job market in China with an increased standard-of-living expectation. These young workers see how others live in high wage countries and the resulting desire for an improved standard of living is driving up wages. With a global supply chain already in place, it becomes relatively easy to move low skill production jobs out of China just as quickly as they moved in.

Without a transformation in the way manufacturers produce goods and deliver services, manufacturers are relegated to chasing the lowest wages, moving production from country to country. They seemingly have no choice, forced out as wage increases due to inflation and government regulation make them un-competitive in their existing plants.

When it comes to executing this transformation, companies don't have to re-invent the wheel. There is a wealth of information available to guide companies on how to improve their processes. The bigger challenge is how to motivate the workforce to change. What's required to successfully move towards ideal production is not a single big change, but hundreds of small changes implemented at all levels by all employees. Combined, these changes have a dramatic effect on costs and lead times.

One methodology has recognized the importance of placing the workforce at the center of a manufacturing transformation: Lean. Lean has done so by recognizing that the people who do the work are the same ones who will originate the ideas for improvement and put them into place.

Lean, a continuous improvement methodology, is built upon three pillars: Purpose, Process and People:

- Purpose: The reason the company exists.

- Process: The method a company uses to add value to its product and services.

- People: The people that participate and improve the process.

Companies applying Lean have the same goal as the production editor of "How It's Made." The production editor cuts away at what the film crew captured until just enough remains to educate the viewer about how a product is made. Lean companies perform a similar act when they analyze their processes with the objective of removing those activities that are not adding value to the customer. Lean's power is in the simplicity of its objective: If an activity adds value – keep it; if it doesn't – eliminate it.

Lean has been steadily growing in popularity over the past two decades. It is a culmination of the many improvements to manufacturing processes that started with Henry Ford who in 1913 integrated an entire production system to produce the famous Model T. The production of the Model T was efficient because there were no changeovers in production. With only one model in one color, the production line could be optimized for that one type of car. In the late 1940's as customers demanded more variety in cars, Toyota recognized there were ways to maintain similar efficiencies in production while offering more choices to their customers. Toyota began creating the tools and techniques to improve production and change from a "push" to a "pull" philosophy where they built cars based on current demand rather than on forecasts. As these ideas matured, they became the basis of the Toyota Production System (TPS). Disciples of the Toyota Production System maintain the same philosophy today, believing it's the people that can improve a company and everything else is a tool to support those efforts.

In 1990 James Womack, Daniel Roos, and Daniel Jones published "The Machine that Changed the World," the first book that completely describes the thought process of Lean. Womack's continued efforts over the past two decades since the book has been published have made Lean the most popular continuous improvement methodology available. In 2007, Industry Week published a survey among manufacturers that ranked Lean as the number one continuous improvement methodology, with 40.5% of respondents using Lean at their companies. Because these techniques apply to all processes, Lean continues to gain popularity as it spreads to other industries such as healthcare and financial services.

Lean thought processes inspire companies to look for improvements in ways that have often never been considered before. This is a reason such significant gains can be realized even in mature and what are thought to be highly efficient processes: Lean follows a process without respect to the functional organization of a company. It uses the neutral eyes of the customer to identify opportunities for improving a process, eliminating the well-meaning but costly localized improvements that benefit one department at the cost of another. Lean has a simple litmus test: If the activity is not adding value to the end customer, find a way to minimize or eliminate it to make product flow easily through production.

While Lean provides significant benefits for companies, it does not deliver these improvements by working employees harder. Since the industrial age began, competition between manufacturers has forced companies to continually find ways to take costs out of their processes. These efforts have often resulted in loss of jobs through automation in order to reduce labor costs, or a faster pace of work to increase throughput and shrink unit cost. In contrast, companies that practice Lean rely on their employees who know the process best to identify unproductive activities and replace them with productive ones. This additional productive time results in higher output with the same pace of production using the same capital equipment. For manufacturers looking to reduce unit cost, especially with limited capital investment, Lean can be the answer.

While companies understand the importance of people to the success of a Lean program, many companies approach their process from an inventory and equipment perspective. This book will instead focus on the workforce and its interaction with the other resources required for production. We follow Graham, a production executive at a manufacturer who is challenged to reduce his company's product unit cost by 10% in a year. Along with Graham's story, we describe ideas, techniques and examples of how manufacturers have changed the way they manage the workforce and then standardize those changes through the use of technology. I hope that Graham's story and the techniques and examples we offer can help you gain similar benefits.

CHAPTER 1

PLACING A VALUE ON THE WORKFORCE

The red light on Graham's Blackberry was blinking. It was just after eight in the evening and he had promised his family no email at night, but Graham knew the board of directors met today for what promised to be a tough meeting and he couldn't resist looking.

"Please stop by first thing in the morning – Spencer."

Getting a message like that from the CEO was not a good sign. Graham was responsible for operations and an offshore competitor had recently lowered pricing in the market by almost 10%. The loss of revenue due to that competitor taking market share had reduced earnings and the stock had dived last quarter.

The next morning Graham checked in with Spencer's assistant and walked into the CEO's office.

"Graham, I was given a choice yesterday: Reduce our unit costs by 10% or pack up the equipment and move this division to China. I need your help here. Do you think 10% is achievable? The board is serious about this. Investors are pressuring them to do something immediately to get the share price up. If we don't come back with a plan, we'll have to announce our intentions to shift production offshore.

Graham's stomach started to churn. This was not the first time he'd been under pressure to reduce costs. The first couple of times weren't too bad. Two years ago the company had completed their strategic sourcing effort which had shaved 5% off material prices and cut inventories by 10%. Last year Graham had the painful task of cutting 10% out of the workforce. Employees were still grumbling about doing more work for the same pay level, but overall they had absorbed it. To go back again and reduce unit costs by 10% was going to be difficult. Even more difficult would be telling everyone their jobs would be moved offshore. Graham told Spencer he would find a way.

The board wanted monthly updates, so Graham had to get started right away and begin showing progress soon. He sat down and started penciling out the drivers of unit cost.

Millions have lost jobs that have moved overseas from high labor cost countries in North America, Australasia and Europe.

Since 2000 more than 5 million manufacturing jobs have disappeared from the United States due to low wage competition and automation. In many industries the jobs have moved to countries where products, including shipping costs can be produced at a lower cost based on wages that are a fraction of those paid in the United States.

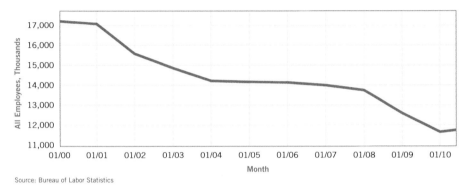

Source: Bureau of Labor Statistics

Manufacturing employment in the United States from 2000 to 2010.

But does an individual who works in China have any more security than an employee in the U.S.? As the cost of living rises in China, countries such as Bangladesh, who pay production employees half of what is paid in China, become the new low cost leaders.

But even manufacturers in Bangladesh are finding that competitive advantage based on low wages is not a sustainable strategy. In its article *"Bangladesh, With Low Pay, Moves In on China,"* The New York Times interviewed Anisul Huq, the former head of the Bangladeshi garment industry's trade group and a factory owner. Commenting on a proposal from the government to increase the monthly wage from the current level of $24, Huq predicts many apparel manufacturers in Bangladesh will go out of business within months if the minimum wage is doubled. Garment workers are demanding an even larger increase of three times the current minimum wage, which is what an experienced worker now earns.

For manufacturers in Bangladesh, the limited transportation infrastructure increases the cost of shipping. The lack of local suppliers requires importing expensive fabric. It's these higher costs that drive factory owners to push down wages to compete with other countries. These businesses have no control over building infrastructure but in a country with limited labor protections, they do have the ability to hire employees at very low wages and keep them depressed. For employees, a low wage job may be a better alternative to no job at all.

Staying globally competitive by driving wages down is not the only answer. In the article, Huq acknowledges that manufacturers in Vietnam are more efficient producers and can afford to pay better wages due to their higher levels of labor productivity. For all manufacturers, higher wages can be supported if productivity is increased.

While companies have limited control over their country's infrastructure or the supplier base, they do have the ability to improve productivity that in turn can support maintaining and even increasing wages. As demonstrated by manufacturers in Vietnam, an increase in labor productivity can eliminate the drive to find the lowest wage employees. These high productivity companies are also more resistant to outside forces such as governments legislating increases in the minimum wage or other employee benefits as was the case in Bangladesh soon after the New York Times article was published.

For most manufacturers this is not a revelation. There has always been a push to increase productivity within manufacturing. But even with those efforts to improve productivity, jobs continue to be lost to lower wage countries. What this trend points to is the larger challenge: While labor may be the most controllable resource for a manufacturer, it is also the most difficult to manage.

Resources such as machines and inventory are inanimate objects with well understood attributes. It's easy to calculate the benefit of reducing inventory in terms of improved cash flow or the return on investment by increasing throughput using automation. When it comes to labor however, the analysis becomes murky. There are many attributes that affect performance and as a result the return on investment is difficult to measure. Understanding the potential in an existing workforce, or in a workforce that is about to be acquired is almost impossible to predict.

For a company that depends on layers of supervisors and managers using manual processes to manage its workforce, the only consistent facts an executive has when it comes to the current value of their workforce is the company's unit labor cost. Similar to any other resource on the balance sheet, the workforce can be analyzed in fiscal terms; value of output divided by cost. There is a price to be paid for this simplification though; the workforce, unlike any other resource, has the ability to innovate and develop new ideas and processes. This value is not described in the general ledger and without additional facts, the value and potential of a workforce is difficult to measure.

The challenge in measuring the value of the workforce does not mean the workforce doesn't offer an opportunity for a company to increase its value. Because different companies manage their workforce with varying degrees of success there is variation on the financial return of an investment in the workforce. Those companies that effectively manage their workforce and the intellectual property (IP) the workforce creates will enjoy higher returns than competitors that don't effectively capture that potential. This return is not easily duplicated. A workforce based competitive advantage is far more valuable than any advantage based on a temporary gain from something available externally in the market. The reason for this is simple. Whoever is providing those external resources will see the value they are delivering and begin marketing those advantages to others. Internally developed intellectual property is much more difficult to duplicate because no one is selling it on the open market. This ability to innovate is a skill and as this skill is used, the workforce gets better at it, increasing the pace and impact of innovation. This workforce driven innovation is a sustainable competitive advantage.

While the workforce is regularly lauded as the most valuable resource within a company, it also holds a more dubious honor. The workforce is the most difficult resource to manage. Here's why:

- Their costs fluctuate without correlated changes in output.

- As a link in a supply chain where predictability translates directly into superior performance, employees are unpredictable.

- While substitutable, employees are not interchangeable.

- Companies are subject to new employee regulations from the government; generally adding cost.

- Turnover and retirement can make a valuable resource disappear overnight.

So while other assets such as machines and materials have predictable costs and performance, the workforce is highly variable in both cost and output. This range of performance presents an opportunity for manufacturers. Companies that reduce the variability of the workforce while still providing a fair and equitable place to work will receive more value from their workforce than those companies that do not. And while inventory costs can only go to zero and a machine can only achieve its theoretical limits of throughput, the new ideas and productivity gains achieved internally through workforce innovation never stop.

The challenge is that managers don't have the luxury of building a labor friendly environment and waiting for the innovation to occur. A company's investors know that the fruits of innovation will be reflected in the unit cost of the company's product or the successfully differentiated offerings that increase revenues. Customers are not patient either. They are buying current value: high quality, shorter lead times, lower unit cost and predictable delivery; not a promise of future excellence.

Graham wrote down the familiar formula for unit cost:

$$\textbf{Unit Cost} = \frac{\text{material} + \text{labor} + \text{overhead}}{\text{units produced}}$$

He promised himself to keep an open mind. Over the last couple of years his team had been using Lean techniques. Some of the results were amazing and others had not worked out.

Because of the time crunch, Graham made some simplifications to the numbers that represented unit cost.

    Revenues = $1,145,000,000

    Material Costs = $350,000,000

    Direct Labor Costs = $200,000,000

    Overhead Costs = $400,000,000

    Units Produced = 500,000

    Employees = 7,000

As he worked through the numbers, Graham started thinking about all the ideas that had been offered and then faded over the years. The proposed gains from many of these ideas seemed too small, the process changes were too big, or a department claimed it would be impacted negatively. For many different reasons these ideas had been shelved.

Graham understood that one of the fundamental advantages of Lean was that rather than focusing on working harder, Lean practitioners look for activities that don't add customer value. The big returns come when those activities are eliminated and the resources are directed toward producing things that customers do value. Recently a consultant came in to provide a seminar and he had offered a new spin on the traditional views of Lean. He suggested that companies had focused too heavily on three of the four M's (Machines, Man, Materials and Methods) of production. While Machines, Materials and Methods were important, too often the changes required of Man (this represents both women and men he explained) were driven by changes made to optimize the other three M's. As the most flexible of all the four M's, the activities of the workforce were designed to accommodate every other resource. If the process is truly changed for the better, this works fine. But when Methods, Materials and Machines are changed and not improved, those costs are not eliminated but rather transferred from the other three M's to Man.

The consultant described a situation where a company purchased lower quality materials from a supplier that still met engineering specifications. As a result the operators had to slow the machines down slightly to obtain high levels of quality. Labor hours per unit were up but the cause was hard to identify because while the material had degraded in quality, it was still within specification. The product designers had optimized the design specifications around functionality, not production cost.

There are many ways that different departments and suppliers lower their costs but really just transfer those costs to production labor. As these inadvertent "cost transfers" accumulate over time, the common denominator is that labor costs increase, negating true productivity gains. This can make it seem like labor costs are increasing while other areas are doing a good job in controlling their costs. As a result labor becomes a lightning rod for targeting cost reductions. Why track down and fix all the contributing factors of cost increases when it is easier to focus on reducing costs by moving the current production processes to a low-wage country and immediately reduce unit cost solely through labor savings?

The consultant had a different approach to this situation. He suggested that rather than trying to identify the contributing costs by looking at the machines, materials and processes, manufacturers should focus on labor to see how they are spending their time creating waste and track it back to the root cause. He called this approach Lean Labor. It was a unique approach because manufacturers always track labor care-

fully when time is spent on value added activities such as production. But indirect labor and non-productive hours are where significant waste can occur, and are typically not measured as accurately.

By extending Lean concepts into Lean Labor, the traditional descriptions of Lean tools and techniques begin to evolve. For example, Taiichi Ohno, Toyota's chief engineer, created seven categories to describe how resources can be wasted. These have evolved into the Seven Wastes of Lean. By viewing these wastes from a workforce perspective, this description can expand to include workforce specific activities. Below is an example of the traditional description of the Seven Wastes of Lean with Lean Labor extensions bolded.

- Transport

    - The unnecessary movement of materials.

    - **Unnecessary movement of people such as call-ins.**

- Inventory

    - Excess inventory not directly required for current orders.

    - **More people than required for current orders.**

- Motion

    - Extra steps taken by employees because of inefficient layout.

    - **Manual paper processes that can be automated such as timekeeping.**

    - Requiring individuals to check information regularly rather than alerting them when action is required.

- Waiting

    - Unexpected delays that extend cycle time and cause the resources such as people and materials to wait unproductively.

    - Processes that build in waiting time. This wait often occurs due to a sub-process that must finish before the main process can start again.

    - Scheduling an individual who is not available due to vacation or previously working in another area.

- Unplanned absenteeism.

- Too few skills or experience to efficiently perform a process.

- Overproduction

  - Making more of something than is required by current orders.

  - Using a person too highly skilled (with corresponding higher pay) for a specific role.

  - Providing too much information to individuals, causing them to search through this detail for the information they require.

- Over Processing

  - Time spent reworking a product or redoing a process.

  - Entering data multiple times into different systems.

  - Decisions that are made, questioned and then reviewed again because of ambiguous supporting information.

- Defects

  - Production that does not conform to expectation.

  - Payment to employees that is not intended.

  - Expired or missing employee skills and certifications that cause quality and performance issues, safety hazards or regulatory infractions.

Reviewing the notes he had taken during the consultant's seminar, Graham was a little skeptical that he would be able to achieve his goal through labor improvements. With an average unit cost of $1,900, direct labor was only 21% of product cost when overhead was included. As he reviewed the consultant's list of wastes, some of the ideas generated within the company that had been previously suggested and discarded came to mind. Graham began listing these ideas, targeting each component of the unit cost, but this time with a focus on labor impact.

Materials

- *Reduce extra inventory required to buffer operations due to labor delays.*

Labor

- *Eliminate errors in calculating payroll.*

- *Eliminate unnecessary labor hours.*

- *Reduce the unplanned or unknown absences.*

- *Improve the labor scheduling processes.*

- *Improve the ability to make decisions on the production floor.*

- *Improve the ability of individuals to react to daily production changes.*

- *Improve safety and compliance to reduce costs and lost time.*

- *Introduce flexible work hours to reduce premium pay.*

Overhead

- *Reduce the time supervisors spend on tracking labor.*

- *Apply Lean to processes outside of production.*

Units produced

- *Reduced labor related machine downtime.*

With Lean Labor a manufacturer doesn't have to possess the advantage of the lowest labor rate in its industry to remain competitive in a global market. The concept is simple: labor is only one of the resources required to manufacture a product. The other two are machines and materials, all combined through a proprietary process. Those companies that understand how to make that combination more productive will reduce their unit costs and lead times beyond a competitor who brings the solitary advantage of low cost labor.

Graham had so far focused on the benefits of Lean Labor as it applies to daily production. What he didn't factor in is one of the outcomes of Lean Labor is a workforce that enjoys an environment that is fair and equitable. It doesn't mean every employee is happy with every rule and its consequences. But knowing all the rules and applying them consistently and transparently means everyone has the same opportunities and this is a critical component of empowering a workforce.

It was now the end of the day and Graham took a look at the list of ideas he had written down. The first one that struck him as an easy target was payments made in error to employees. He wasn't quite sure how big that could be, he had never had an error in his paycheck and the special checks and petty cash he approved were always for legitimate errors the company had made in calculating pay. But the idea came from payroll and admittedly, he hadn't thought much about it.

Graham made a call and set up a meeting the next morning with the director of payroll.

CHAPTER 2

DELIVERING THE
PERFECT PAYCHECK

■■■■

The next morning the payroll director had several reports prepared for Graham. The one that got his attention right away was the average wage chart for the last three years. What struck him was that each year the actual average wage was creeping up.

"I've seen this before but always attributed it to increased overtime because we cut back headcount. Why do you think these are costs that we can control?" Graham asked.

The payroll director said she had thought the same thing at first, but after she had tracked down a couple of specific timecards, and spoke with several payroll administrators and supervisors she had come across several anecdotes that had changed her mind. Supervisors were interpreting pay rules which led to inadvertently paying their employees too much. Some individuals were taking advantage of the premium pay rules to increase their pay. There was also one story she heard that got her upset: People were gaming and cheating their timecards to add a little pay without working for it or working a little less time for the same pay.

"Each instance was small and it's spread out across departments so no individual event seemed big enough to cause alarm." she continued. "Also, my team sees these, but because of headcount reductions, the few of us left are under a time crunch to get payroll processed at the end of each pay period. If I started using overtime to go back and fix the errors, the company would lose the money we just saved through the headcount reduction."

"Small is the new big in my book!" exclaimed Graham. "These seem like they should be easy to fix and converting a couple of percent of wasted payroll dollars into effective production puts us on the right track to achieving our goal of achieving a reduction of 10% in unit costs."

If employee paychecks were considered a product line, it would rank as one of the largest products at most companies. But as an expense, rarely is it given the same level of operational scrutiny as a revenue-producing product. Like a utility such as electricity or water, payroll is expected to be on time and accurate, with managers only paying attention when something goes awry. While companies are heavily focused on efficiency and effectiveness in their main value-add processes, what they don't realize is that just the mistakes made by producing a paycheck inefficiently can inflate payroll on average by 2.4%.

By looking for inefficiencies across the workforce rather than by the labor associated with a product, companies can eliminate significant amounts of payroll waste that will flow right to profits.

Applying the same principles of work standardization, a company can realize proven benefits in terms of reduced payroll cost, increased time for supervisors and payroll administrators, improved employee (and in this case they are the customer) morale and less exposure to compliance risk. Collectively these ideas serve one purpose. And that's to deliver the *Perfect Paycheck.*

The Perfect Paycheck has three components:

- **The right pay...** Paychecks that are more or less than earned are caused by many reasons from mistaken interpretation of pay rules and calculation errors to employee abuse. The perfect paycheck accurately pays an employee for the hours worked as intended by the company and expected by the employee.

- **At the right price...** The timekeeping and payroll process winds through many different departments. Edits and approvals are required by many people to process payroll. As a result, it can be difficult to determine exactly how much producing a paycheck really costs a company. The Perfect Paycheck process automates the repetitive actions and calls attention to conditions and decisions that need attention. As a result, the cost to produce a paycheck is minimized.

- **Delivered at the right time...** In addition to government regulations requiring on-time payment of taxes and payroll, employees are personally dependent on receiving their paychecks on time. Similar to a late order that is sped up through the use of overtime and premium freight to meet an important due date, the payroll process can be sped up as well. Just like accelerating an order, there is a cost to speed up the timekeeping and payroll process. However, with timekeeping and payroll the costs are not easy to measure and usually result in unearned pay for employees. The perfect paycheck provides a repeatable process that limits time-wasting variability.

There are three main categories that provide the best return on investment when it comes to improving the timekeeping and payroll process. First is to automate manual processes within the timekeeping system by taking steps such as eliminating paper forms, no longer entering information into multiple systems and calculating values automatically rather than manually. Second is to eliminate gray areas that cause interpretation in pay and accrual policies. Third, weakness in the processes should be eliminated. These weaknesses allow some employees to game or abuse the system, which lead to higher pay without corresponding increases in output.

Using Lean Tools to Improve the Timekeeping Process

Fortunately, the same tools that are used to improve production processes can be used to improve the timekeeping and payroll process. From Value Stream Maps to Ishikawa (Fishbone) diagrams, these tools can uncover wasted time and root cause issues.

Here's an example of a company that utilized a value stream map to uncover waste and implemented a new process and technology to automate and streamline the time-keeping process.

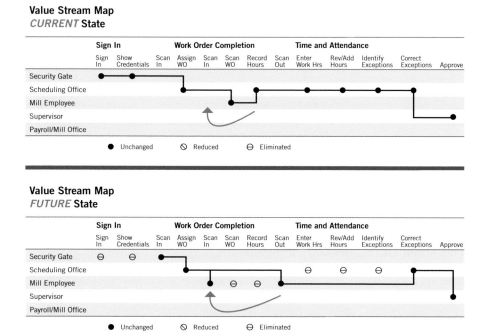

An example of a value stream map developed to analyze the labor tracking process at a paper products company.

This paper products company analyzed each step of its time and work order tracking process and was able to find ways to eliminate duplication and eliminate steps by using automation technology.

Through its analysis, the company identified lost hours each week. Implementing some of the techniques in this and following chapters, it was able to put that time back to value-add activities and generated a healthy return on its investment.

Why Payroll Tends to Increase Over Time without Additional Worked Hours

There is one main difference between the Perfect Paycheck and another common manufacturing goal, achieving the Perfect Order:

The feedback companies receive on product quality.

Manufacturers receive feedback on almost every defect. It comes in the form of returns, repairs, discount requests, managing an unhappy customer, or in the subtlest but most damaging form, a drop in sales. Companies can measure the cost of providing poor quality service and product.

Unlike the customer of a company's products, the payroll customer (in this case, the employee receiving the paycheck) is only reporting about half the defects he finds.

Of all the special checks written and retro-active pay edits made a year, how many are due to the money returned from the employee to the company? And of those, did the employee volunteer that information?

Of course not. There are very few situations where an employee notices a small amount of extra pay and will voluntarily return it. But we all know what happens when they are accidentally underpaid. The employee will bring it to his supervisor's and payroll's attention and request the difference. Over time, this silently inflates pay without a corresponding increase in productive output from the workforce. This is commonly referred to as "payroll inflation."

While this is not a flattering picture of the company's most valuable asset, its employees, the onus is not on the employees to report a company's mistakes. The responsibility lies with the company to effectively manage the timekeeping and payroll process.

Imagine if a company learned it was including 3% more product in customer shipments than was being ordered and paid for. The company wouldn't penalize the customer, it would correct the process and eliminate the excess product.

To understand how this happens at the employee and paycheck level, take a look at an approximation of the distribution of payroll errors shown in the following graph. When pay is too low; through miscalculation or interpretation of a pay rule, one can be sure the employee receiving the reduced paycheck will be in the payroll department looking for the missed compensation.

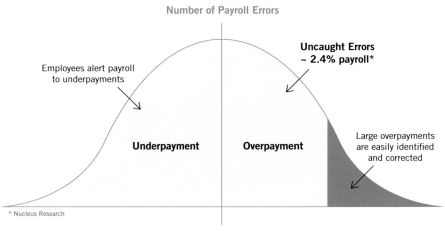

Number of Payroll Errors

Uncaught Errors
~ 2.4% payroll*

Employees alert payroll
to underpayments

Underpayment   **Overpayment**

Large overpayments
are easily identified
and corrected

* Nucleus Research

Amount of payroll error

Distribution of payroll errors among a population of employees.

Occasionally there are significant overpayments such as a misplaced decimal point or a missed time stamp that implies someone worked through the night. But these types of errors are quickly caught when someone notices there were 16 extra hours of overtime paid or if a $20,000 paycheck is issued.

In the middle of those obvious errors lies the difficult area. On a weekly basis, there is legitimate variability in pay due to overtime, call-ins, shift premiums, missed breaks and lunches, and requested changes in worked hours. The question is how much error has to occur before someone can tell the difference between normal variation of earned pay and a mistake? Two hours, three hours?

The employee has the advantage here. The employee knows the detail of every pay rule that applies to him and is familiar with his hours worked. A supervisor or payroll administrator may be reviewing dozens or hundreds of timecards, all with different situations.

To get a sense of what this overpayment could cost a company, say 15% of a 1000 employee workforce has their pay inflated through errors in the process. Some may also take advantage of loosely enforced pay rules. For this exercise, let's say that as a result of those errors and loosely enforced rules they are paid for two hours they did not work. For those 150 employees, the two paid, but not earned hours a week at an hourly wage of $20 results in a company overpaying those employees by almost $300,000 annually.

Over the course of time, employees realize they can win arguments about gray areas in pay policies as they file grievances or argue with supervisors about interpretations of how hours should be compensated. Supervisors learn where they lose arguments and begin automatically calculating pay in favor of employees. These decisions build precedent within the organization and spread through departments. As a result, payroll increases in areas that were not originally intended when the pay policy was first written.

This and similar situations occur in three different categories within the timekeeping process: Manual processes and undefined pay situations, employee abuse of gaps in timekeeping procedures and supervisors bending the rules to help favored employees.

Manual Processes and Undefined Pay Situations

Manual Timekeeping Processes

Let's face it; managing timecards is not high on anyone's list of favorite things to do. And the faster employees, supervisors and payroll administrators can get through completing, checking and approving timecards each pay period the better. Unfortunately, when a process is manual, the shortcuts people take to move quickly through the timekeeping process results in errors.

Think about a supervisor who at the end of the pay period now has 10, 20 or more timecards to review. On a weekly pay period this means 20 to 40 time stamps per employee. With a basic timecard, there is not much information to assist that supervisor in getting through those timecards quickly and accurately.

Time Card

| Employee | John Doe (Employee # 12344) | | Manager: | | |

Extension: x5072
Week ending: 9/24/2010

Day	Date	In	Out	Overtime	Total
Monday	9/18/2010	7:33 AM	11:29 AM		3:56
Monday	9/18/2010	12:03 AM	3:58 PM		3:55
Tuesday	9/19/2010	7:48 AM	11:25 AM		3:37
Tuesday	9/19/2010	11:59 AM	4:10 PM		4:11
Wednesday	9/20/2010	7:28 AM	11:29 AM		4:01
Wednesday	9/20/2010	12:01 PM	3:56 AM		3:46
Thursday	9/21/2010	7:36 AM	11:31 AM		3:55
Thursday	9/21/2010	12:01 PM	6:01 PM	2	6:00
Friday	9/22/2010	7:31 AM	11:15 AM		3:44
Friday	9/22/2010	11:54 AM	4:03 PM		4:09
Saturday	9/223/2010				
Sunday	9/24/2010				
Total Hours					**41.25**

Employee signature   Date

Manager signature   Date

Typical weekly timecard of a single employee.

With lots of time stamps and only summary information, unless the hours are really out of line, a supervisor has to make a judgment call. Should he spend the time chasing down the reason for an extra 15 minutes here and there or approve them and get back to the latest fire on the production line? Most will choose their main job, running a production line. The decision making process is simple: This extra time might be legitimate anyway, and if it isn't, the supervisor is in for an argument with the employee. Depending on how tightly managed the labor dollars are in the company, there may not be any consequence for letting a couple of extra hours slide through.

As time passes, employees and supervisors fall into a comfortable pattern of knowing what the limits are and what raises flags. Everyone adjusts their behavior toward that norm. Thus begins a slow cycle of payroll inflation as supervisors rationalize that their time is more productively spent managing the business rather than managing timecards.

And this cycle is exactly where technology can both reduce payroll errors and make a supervisor's life easier.

5S is an example of a Lean technique that can be applied to the timekeeping process. 5S is most often considered when organizing physical workspaces. It is a technique described by the following 5 terms: sort, store, shine, standardize and sustain. One technique within 5S that production operators are taught is to prioritize the location of their tools ensuring that the ones they need most are closest at hand. Those that are rarely used are put away so they don't take up valuable space or get dirty. This same technique can be applied to timecards and payroll processing workflows.

By making the timekeeping interface and process easy to use, employees and supervisors will perform their work more effectively. These changes to the interface include signaling the supervisor when something needs to be done, such as an alert to check a time-off request or address an employee attendance issue. Details that justify a change in scheduled hours can be linked to the timestamp making it easy to understand the change. These changes reduce the "set-up and processing" time for timekeeping interactions. As a result, supervisors can update and approve events daily, moving to a flow rather than batch process when managing timecards. The advantage of improved flow is threefold. First, memories of events are clearer when they are re-called in the same day. Secondly, the updated information provided by one department means another department such as Human Resources can also improve the flow of its work rather than receiving a large batch of information at the end of a pay period. Finally, employee morale is improved as their requests for time off and other interactions with the company are responded to quickly. This might allow the employee to book travel a little sooner resulting in personal savings.

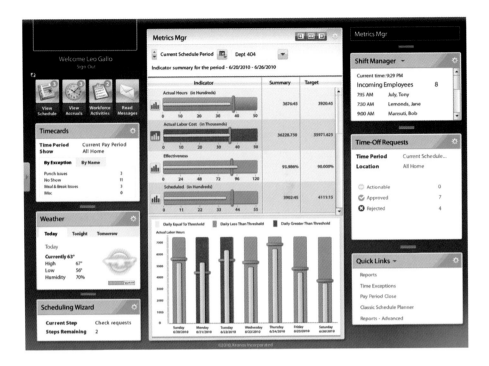

The image above shows an interface that highlights only the actions required by a supervisor in the upper left corner. This organization of the information gets supervisors in and out of the application quickly, but details are still available on the sidebars should they be needed.

In addition to organization of information, there are several underlying causes of payroll inflation, including the manual interpretation of pay rules, employee abuse of time and poor decisions by supervisors.

Manual Interpretation of Pay Rules

Some pay rules are simple....weekly overtime for example. An employee works more than forty hours in a week and receives 1.5 times average wage during that pay period for those extra hours. Other simple pay rules are examples of premium pay such as 1.5 times the base wage for coming in when the employee wasn't scheduled or two times base wage for working a holiday that wasn't scheduled.

Pay rules are added to hours and wage calculations for a number of reasons. Notably federal and state regulations such as the U.S. Fair Labor Standard Act (FLSA) that governs basic overtime, U.S. state regulations such as California's meal and break rules or the European working time directive that governs average working time and breaks. Companies also add their own pay rules to encourage flexibility in the workforce or to reward employees for working more difficult or less-desirable jobs.

These pay rules accumulate over time. And because they are often written into multiple contracts and regulations, a few simple pay rules can be combined in ways that weren't previously considered and result in situations where multiple pay rules apply to one time span.

To see how this can occur and why it would cause a problem, consider the following situation where an employee planned to work only 32 hours (four days) and take a scheduled holiday off on Friday.

Imagine in this example that someone calls in sick, and our employee was asked to come in and work on that holiday. Because it was busy, not only did she work the eight hours that was scheduled, but also worked an additional two hours for a total of 10 hours on Friday.

The following are two methods for calculating her pay for the week.

Method One

1. 32 hours regular pay

2. 8 hours holiday pay

3. Double time for 8 hours of unscheduled "call-in" Friday

4. Apply the overtime rate of 1.5 on the current double time rate for the 2 hours over 40 earned on Friday

This method results in a total of 62 hours of pay.

Method Two

In this method, the supervisor interprets the pay policy so that employees are only eligible for a single premium at any time no matter what the situation, resulting in the following.

1.   32 hours regular pay

2.   8 hours holiday pay

3.   Double time for 8 hours of unscheduled "call in" Friday

4.   Double time rate for the 2 hours over 40 worked on Friday because that is higher than the 1.5 multiplier of standard overtime pay

This method results in a total of 60 hours of pay.

The fact that there are two viable options to calculate pay for this employee presents a dilemma for both employees and supervisors. Supervisors trying to maintain a motivated workforce, stay in compliance with company policy, and control a labor budget are challenged. The employee is going to favor the higher pay scenario and if the situation isn't documented, may file a grievance if the decision doesn't go her way. Supervisors can also use the two options inconsistently between employees. For example, would the supervisor support the employee's version of how she should be paid if the employee did him a favor by coming in to work when the supervisor was short-handed?

Which pay calculation was intended by the company? Will all supervisors and payroll personnel calculate it the same way?

The company is now inconsistent in its pay and accrual practices and is sometimes over-paying, or worse, underpaying and liable for that extra pay plus fines due to labor laws.

Manual Tracking of Paid Time Off

This is an area that applies to both exempt and non-exempt employees. The issue occurs in the accuracy of paid time off that accrues based on the time an employee works. It also includes unpaid time off such as absences allowed through the Family Medical Leave Act (FMLA). FMLA is a U.S. federal regulation administered by the Department of Labor designed to provide a method for employees to take unpaid time off for certain medical and family reasons. It protects the employee's job and continues health benefits during the time off. Some companies provide continued pay for certain types of leave such as maternity leave, and health benefit costs may shift from employer to employee depending on the length of leave. There are two types of losses in this category. The first is accuracy in tracking, calculation and visibility throughout the organization which we'll cover next. Employee abuse of FMLA is the second and will be covered later in the chapter.

When time-off requests are made manually, several departments will touch the information. The employee's supervisor must check and approve, HR will update accrual records and Payroll will adjust the paycheck based on the type of leave. As people's plans change, all this updated information must be transmitted throughout the organization again increasing workload and the likelihood that a mistake will be made. The second issue arises in that supervisors must evaluate the number of people taking time off at once. If too many people take time off at once, production will be impacted. As a result there are often policies in place providing rules around prioritization of leave requests. Even after the leave has been approved, communication of the leave to others who depend on that employee must be communicated. A calendar on the wall with people's names written over their days of absences may not be enough.

A third area of loss is in calculating the appropriate pay for the specific type of absence. Not all types of absence are paid the same way. Regulations and company policy dictates how pay is handled over the duration of the absence. For longer term absence taken under FMLA guidelines, companies often provide different levels of pay and benefits based on the duration of absence. For example, a company may pay its employees during this time by having them use up accrued time first such as their vacation and paid sick time. After this runs out the employee is then paid short term disability and finally long term disability. Shared health benefit costs may also be fully transferred to the employee at some point. Without an automated method of cascading through these pay codes as the absence continues, a payroll clerk must check the status of every absent employee, look up their accrued time, know the policy and make a manual adjustment to pay when required.

Safety and Other Work Based Policies

As an extension to 5S, there is a sixth S often added. It represents safety. In addition to accurate pay, employee actions regarding safety can cause harm to others or themselves. These actions can also generate unnecessary expense for a company. Safety incidents along with other work based policies such as performance and failing to take direction are often tracked manually. In addition to providing supervisor latitude for tracking and addressing issues, a manual record makes it difficult to identify common issues across many employees and provide auditable records for grievances. The ability to easily analyze historical records provides companies with accident patterns that can be corrected through changes to work practices and processes. The largest resulting benefit is an improved work environment for employees. There is also a measurable financial benefit associated with that improvement in safety. In one recent case, a manufacturer that employs a significant number of welders tracked and analyzed their electronic employee safety records over time as well as the cost of each incident. In performing the analysis it identified that a majority of its safety incidents were eye related. By making changes to its work procedures it was able to reduce those incidents by 40%. With an auditable trail that incidents were down and the ability to show that the change in practice reduced the potential for future accidents, the company was also able to reduce its medical insurance premiums by $2 million annually.

Employee Abuse of Paid Time

This is often a sensitive subject. Many supervisors have a strong relationship with their employees and do not want to start a discussion that leads to realizing that employees are abusing paid time. Additionally, in what are otherwise great employees, some of these abuses are relatively innocent. A couple of minutes idling to ensure a full 30 minutes are paid or the occasional buddy punch when someone is running late is rationalized away. The employee figures that they have provided extra work to the company at some other time and all is now fair. For most companies regular time abuse is confined to only a small percentage of employees, so increasing control for everyone due to the behavior of a few can have unintended consequences for the entire workforce.

Unfortunately this adds up. Entire workforce management software applications have paid for themselves when the system put an end to paid but un-earned hours. Because it is hidden cost, the magnitude of the savings is often a complete surprise to management.

The good news is that used appropriately, this technology does not punish employees who follow work and pay policies. It only identifies and stops those abusing the policies. This is why it has been so effective with so many companies. It can, in fact, improve morale because the majority of the employees following the rules now see they are being treated equitably.

The following are some common methods of time and pay abuse that have been experienced by a wide variety of companies.

"Tradesies"

Even well written pay rules can be gamed and manipulated. Over time, companies, especially those with collective bargaining or workers' council agreements in place, will add more pay rules to address certain circumstances. These rules are often premiums that will be paid for situations such as coming in when an employee is not scheduled or paying a premium for working the third shift. In many cases, these pay rules can overlap, causing a pyramid effect resulting in hourly pay that is multiples over the base rate.

Are employees aware of the intricacies? Of course they are. They understand the compensation plan and behave accordingly. Impacting employee behavior is why the company put the plan in place.

But the company didn't intend for employees to begin to manipulate the way they work in order to increase their hourly rate. This practice is affectionately known as "Tradesies" in parts of Western Canada. "Tradesies" occur when employees study the pay rules and then collude to trade shifts in order to maximize their pay. This results in the unintended consequence of increased payroll without an increase in output or flexibility of the workforce.

"Tradesies" is certainly not what management intended when they were mapping out the rules. Because there are no extra worked hours it's extremely difficult to track this abuse down. It just results in larger labor cost variances when reconciling paid hours to worked hours. Eventually this variance winds its way into overhead costs and is distributed across all products and services.

These situations can be identified by running audit reports of how pay rules are applied to specific time spans for an individual. This will identify which employees are regularly earning multiple premiums in unintended ways.

Buddy Punching or Fraudulent Clocking

This is a time honored tradition for many employees. It can start off relatively innocently.

"We're running a little late, I'll park the car, can you swipe my badge? I'll be there in a minute."

Over time, if employees are not called out for this behavior, what was once an exception now becomes embedded in the company's culture. It's not just one person and a minute or two to park the car, but 10 or 15 minutes on a more regular basis among an increasing segment of the employees.

The simplest way to eliminate buddy punching is through the use of the simple finger scan or biometrics. A finger scan ensures the person clocking in is who they claim to be. Occasionally fought by individuals and unions, it is absolutely the most effective way to stop buddy punching. One company recently reported at a Workforce Management User Conference that when its first building was outfitted with new biometric terminals, the other buildings within a 100 mile radius suddenly experienced a significant drop in labor hours. This occurred as a result of the news that the company was beginning to look at hours more closely and was installing terminals that would eliminate buddy punching. This is a nice example of the Hawthorne effect, (a positive reaction in behavior and productivity from people when they become aware they are being measured) ... and the power of biometrics.

This is as good a time as any to dispel a relatively common myth and the number one stated reason for employee and union protest against biometrics and privacy concerns: The finger scan technology used in most terminals is not a fingerprint. What occurs when a fingerprint is initially scanned into the timekeeping system is an algorithm processes the scan and saves just enough points of data on the scan to match against a fingerprint on a subsequent scan. By matching those points back to the person's fingerprint as they place their finger on the scanning device, the device can confirm their identity with high certainty. An important component of the algorithm is those data points cannot be used to re-create a finger print. So there is no security or privacy issue from having finger scan data stored in a timekeeping or other system.

Gaming the Clock

When it comes to tracking an employee's time companies have two options. First, they can track it to the minute and pay exactly what the timecard shows. But this has its drawbacks. Calculations and timecard processing can be tedious because everything is calculated to the minute. Government legislation around the world such as the U.S.'s Federal Labor Standards Act (FLSA) establishes standards for minimum wages, overtime, recordkeeping and child labor. FLSA is a U.S. federal law, administered by the Wage and Hour division of the Department of Labor. It covers several areas of timekeeping and in this case states that companies have to pay employees based on the details of the time record.

When an employee clocks in a couple of minutes early each day and then gets on the end of the line as employees clock out each day, he can earn an hour of overtime each week without providing any incremental output for those wages. Because of legislation the employer has no choice but to pay.

FLSA provides employers with another option. Companies can apply rounding rules to timestamps. In effect this "rounds" an actual timestamp forward or backward to the nearest increment of time set by the company. Often this is measured in tenths of an hour. So a timestamp that reads 3:06 PM is calculated as 3:00 PM. This makes it easier to calculate and process payroll. It is also designed to support the fluctuations that take place during clocking in and out so companies and employees are neither penalized nor rewarded for being at the front or end of a line during the beginning or end of day. This rounding of timestamps also applies to meals and breaks.

The intent of the law is not to reward or penalize either employee or companies, but rather simplify the timekeeping process for everyone. Unfortunately, there are ways to game this rule to increase pay without working or to work fewer hours at their current pay. Some employees will adjust their habits to always clock in a couple of minutes late (and the time will be adjusted back) and then clock out a couple of minutes early (the time will be adjusted forward.)

With this behavior, an employee can add 12 minutes of paid but un-worked time to each pair of timestamps. And for employees that clock in and out for lunch and two breaks a day, the four pairs of timestamps represent up to 48 minutes of paid but un-worked time each day.

Employees will also test the boundaries of company policy and enforcement by clocking in seven minutes before the hour and clocking out seven minutes after the hour to increase their pay but only work their scheduled hours. Even worse, this will be calculated as overtime because they've worked more than 40 hours.

It's not the supervisors fault if they don't catch all of these. Just do the arithmetic: There are one million or more clock ins and outs occurring per thousand employees annually if employees track their lunch break. Any one of these can be an opportunity for an employee to extend their paid but not worked time by a couple of minutes.

Is every supervisor really looking at each of these punches, determining if it is un-scheduled and unjustified? Experience has shown that rounding rule abuse is similar to the payroll error distribution curve shown previously. A timestamp that provides a large enough payout will "trip the alarms" when a supervisor is reviewing time, but the majority of smaller inconsistencies in an employee's timestamps go unnoticed and take too much effort to track down.

After looking at the actual clock records over a period of time, many employers have found that employees have much more control over their clock in and out times than was previously thought. They find that when employees are clocking in and out of work for the day, they are heavily favoring clocking in six minutes after the hour and clocking out six minutes before the hour. While this doesn't seem like too much time at the individual level, when 10% of the employees are taking 10 minutes a day (five minutes each time they clock in or out), at a wage of $20/hour that adds up to more than $74,000 per thousand employees annually in time paid but not worked. Even worse, there is also the negative impact on the morale of the other employees who see this happening. Production can also be impacted if others are dependent on that person.

While there are many stories about how this gaming occurs in different companies, one of the more dramatic in terms of the differences of rules and subsequent pay between plants within one company comes from a large food processer. It had acquired plants and distribution centers in many states over time and had inherited several different pay policies. Some plants had rounding rules and others paid exactly what the timestamps accumulated. After installing a centralized timekeeping system, an enterprising IT analyst developed reports to look at the different behaviors at the different plants. He noticed that where there were no rounding rules, pay was significantly higher than where rounding rules were in place. Employees were taking advantage by a few minutes a day punching in just a little early and punching out just a little late. He calculated that by standardizing the rounding rules across all plants the company could reduce payroll by $500,000 across 8,000 employees annually. And that was without any change in clock times, only in the way the timestamps were rounded. Needless to say, a standardized policy was implemented across all plants as soon as the company was able.

One method to control improper clocking is to put restrictions on the time-collection device and only allow employees to clock in and out based on their schedules. These can be over-ridden by a supervisor either at the device or by changing the schedule for a day, due to an individual's needs.

Another method of controlling this behavior is to signal when it's time to transition from one task to the next. This eliminates the excuse of employees either leaving their station too early or too late in order to hide the fact they are "gaming the clock."

To help employees and supervisors know the appropriate time to start cleaning at the end of the shift, one company sounds a bell triggered by the time clock 15 minutes before the end of the shift. This signals the employees so they know when to stop production and begin cleaning up for the day. This signal (or andon) eliminates the variability of one person starting to clean up 30 minutes early, disrupting production, and another starting five minutes before the end of the shift and claiming to need overtime.

One other company was more creative about its application of rounding rules. Rather than provide a six-minute window on either side of a timestamp, it measured the actual variation of timestamps and narrowed down the window to three minutes. Because there was a historical record of employees' timestamps to demonstrate this window of three minutes was achievable, it's tough to argue the need for a six minute window.

Other companies have provided the six-minute window based on the total time of the pair of punches. So if an employee clocks out for a 30 minute break five minutes early and clocks back in three minutes late, the actual break time is 38 minutes. Rather than rounding to 30 minutes as would be calculated if each timestamp was rounded individually, the company totals the total time taken for break and then rounds that value which results in a 40 minute break. The ability to round this way can vary from state to state based on local laws.

How do companies deal with the complexity of managing timestamps when there are so many to evaluate? Clearly written policies are a good start. Automating those policies will remove the extra effort and emotional stress required by supervisors in monitoring and making interpretations. As a result payroll will decrease.

Attendance, Accrued Time Off and Other Event Based Absence Policies

Abuse in this category can take several forms. The simplest is the failure to report time off. Every industry has stories about employees who retire with over a year's worth of accrued vacation and sick pay. With no records over the years about attendance and paper forms for all employees' vacation requests long gone, there is little recourse for the company but to pay the employee. This can be a surprising liability for many companies because they did not accrue funds for this paid time. To resolve this situation, many companies have put policies in place that automatically retire unused vacation and sick days each year.

A second type of abuse occurs more intermittently during the course of an employee's tenure. Predictable resources are a cornerstone of efficient manufacturing. But when employees unexpectedly don't show for work, production processes are disrupted just as though material didn't arrive or a machine broke down.

These absences include not showing up at work, and gaming regulations such as the Family Medical Leave Act (FMLA) or Working Time Directives through abuse of intermittent leave rights.

Because the unplanned absence directly affects the primary value-added process, supervisors have to react. They have several options, but none are as good as the original plan to have the employee present when he is scheduled. In addition there's a lag in time when it's not known if the person is a little late or not coming in at all. Once the supervisor makes a decision to move forward without the person there's a continued lag in production while the supervisor finds a replacement, either through moving someone from a different department, offering overtime to someone from the previous shift, calling someone else in or doing the work himself. Worse, if the missing skill is critical, the other employees may have to find other work for that shift.

In all cases, this unplanned absenteeism has added waste to the process, either through waiting, overpaying someone else to do the work, or by performing work that wasn't needed.

Changing behavior is always difficult, but there are some strong reasons for actively managing attendance. The challenge is creating policies that encourage high levels of attendance while providing the flexibility a workforce needs to balance their own lives outside of work. If management doesn't create and enforce a policy, the workplace culture will define one for the company. An undefined or unenforced policy is not efficient and the losses show up in one of two ways, excess labor cost or reduced employee morale.

Unmanaged absenteeism is often resolved by supervisors in one of the three following ways. Supervisors use these techniques because they are typically not measured as closely as production metrics such as inventory levels or late orders.

- Overstaffing everyday to accommodate the percentage of absenteeism they expect.

- Use of overtime to fill an open shift.

- Substitution of an over-skilled individual to perform the work.

It's not as easy to quantify the second type of cost, reduced morale, as it is to quantify excess labor costs. But even though it is difficult to quantify, it is just as real. Reduced morale leads to decreased productivity and less innovation.

Reduced morale starts innocently enough. Depending on the country, opening day of deer or fishing season or the day after the big football game are well known for having high levels of unplanned absence. Their absence means more work for those who show up on those days. For those who come to work but had requested the time off and were denied, it can be frustrating to see others get away with this behavior. When policies aren't enforced fairly it can have a serious impact on morale. This situation also puts supervisors in the position of being "the bad guy." Once employees realize there is some latitude on enforcing the attendance policy, they will pressure supervisors to let the unexcused absence or tardy arrival slide. Maybe the employee won't accept overtime the next time they are needed. One technique companies use to help supervisors enforce company policy is to automate the disciplinary steps. This removes the discretion from the supervisor and lets the software take the "heat" for enforcing absence and other policy infractions. That being said, automation won't fix a bad policy and rewarding good behavior is just as important as disciplining bad behavior.

Employee absence is a difficult area to manage because there is a need to balance an employee's personal needs, government regulation such as the Family Medical Leave Act or European Maternity and Paternity legislation and the need of the business to have employee resources available.

Understanding patterns of use and abuse in a specific company along with knowledge about government regulations can help develop a leave policy that meets everyone's needs and provide data for enforcing policies. Here are some ways policies can be modified to limit abuse:

- Collecting reasons for absenteeism will provide patterns that can be used as a factual discussion point during a disciplinary discussion.

- Calculating FMLA absence on a rolling 12 months rather than on a calendar year can eliminate "clock resetting" at the beginning of the year.

- Ensuring an absence policy includes providing reasonable notice of leave and documenting whether that notice was provided.

Reading the regulations and consulting with your company's attorney will often uncover methods your company can use to provide protection against employee abuse.

While absence is a major factor in disruption of production and a driver of increased labor costs, there are many other "on-the-job" event based situations that can also increase costs and reduce morale. Performance issues, failure to use safety devices, theft of materials or tools, and failure to accept assignments all must be tracked and enforced consistently. Some of these events such as injury are required to be reported to health and safety authorities such as Occupational Safety and Health Administration (OSHA) or Health and Safety Executive (HSE). Automating the enforcement of absence, attendance and on-the-job policies help ensure that supervisors are able to deliver fair and equitable treatment to employees, reduce the paperwork burden and provide an audit trail to past events.

Assuring Supervisors are Fair in Addition to Being Equitable

Fairness (conforming to the policies of the company) and equity (treating employees who are in similar situations the same way) are the foundation of an empowered workforce. Employees that feel they are being treated unfairly are not spending their time thinking of ways to improve a company. They are frustrated and at best fuming silently. At worst they are distracting others through their complaints. Supervisors have been charged with a trust and responsibility in managing their team. But for some this power has been used arbitrarily outside of company policy in order to maintain the supervisor's own version of fairness when dealing with employees.

One example is editing a timecard after the fact. An employee may come in late regularly. If the supervisor wants to hide that from management as well as ensure the employee receives the pay for missed time, an edit is made to the timecard details. In manual and basic timekeeping systems, these edits are final and the original record is lost. But in current systems, these timecards edits have complete details that can be viewed easily during an audit showing details such as the reason for change, original timestamp value, new timestamp value, and who actually made the change. Edits to time cards are a regular occurrence. But with the millions of timestamps to evaluate and the thousands of edits that occur, identifying the fraudulent ones can be challenging.

If there is suspicion of abuse, an audit of a timekeeping system can provide clues that highlight suspicious behaviors. The number of edits by a supervisor is a good indicator. Are there inconsistencies where one or two supervisors have many more edits than others? Are there patterns in these edits such as regularly changing a "late in" to an "on time"? Is one person's time card being edited more than others? Are they typically favorable edits to the employee?

Sweetheart Scheduling

Supervisors can also have an impact on cost performance and morale through the practice of "sweetheart scheduling". This involves a supervisor providing preferential treatment in terms of jobs, days or overtime assigned to an individual or group of employees, resulting in an unfair allocation of work and pay. Many companies have rules in place for assigning discretionary work such as overtime or rotating through shifts. To assist in these decisions, there are techniques (and tools) to ensure equity. One is known as Overtime Equalization. This technique ensures everyone is equally offered (but doesn't have to accept) opportunities for overtime. The offer is often based on seniority for employees qualified to perform the work. The rules are known, the allocation is equitable, and the decisions are visible and auditable for all to see.

Achieving the Perfect Paycheck

These are some of the largest areas of waste when it comes to delivering the Perfect Paycheck. But there are other areas in the human resources role that can also be explored for waste: benefits administration, onboarding new hires, time-off requests, transferring employees, adjusting wages and removing terminated employees from the active records. To quickly estimate how much opportunity for improvement there is at a company, identify how many times a person's name or ID has to be re-entered when entering information about him. Each time is an opportunity for simplification.

Considering that most people think of the payroll department as simply a timecard and a paycheck producing process, the daily complexity can be surprising. By applying Lean and Six Sigma tools to the process and automating with technology, these processes can be made more efficient and repeatable, resulting in the Perfect Paycheck.

Because the deficiencies are often known but hidden to management, the next step can be to hold a kaizen event. (A kaizen event is a gathering of people who participate in a specific process to think of ways to make the process simpler, reduce wasted efforts and increase quality.) Include the people who are filling out timecards and those approving them along with the people in payroll who process timecards. An example of this type of event occurred several years ago at a manufacturer of industrial gases that had a distributed production and delivery environment. What began as a simple process defined by a few sticky notes on the wall had soon expanded to cover the wall as people began sharing how they handled all the exceptions and decisions that occurred in their particular work areas.

Over the years, people with good intentions had built in undocumented processes to ensure that paychecks were delivered on time. They had tried to get issues resolved but for a variety of reasons, weren't able to make progress. As a result they adjusted what was in their control to get the job done. One example of good intentions increasing company payroll was that payroll employees had started coming in at five in the morning for several days after the pay period ended. They needed the extra time in order to accommodate all the paperwork and chasing down of missing information. But in this effort, they had built in extra overtime hours that could be eliminated with a well defined, automated process.

In these kaizen events people from different functional areas realize the impact they have on others or the duplication of work that is occurring. As they analyze the complete process together, not just the portion that occurs within their respective departments, the waste becomes evident.

There is one other important reason that the Perfect Paycheck is an important aspect of manufacturing. Governments have created laws to aid in enforcing the rights of employees. All countries require some level of compliance to pay rules. From the India Factory Act to the Chinese Employment Law each country has its unique rules governing pay and employment. Governments enforce these laws through agencies that have the power to inspect plants and audit labor and employment records. Even innocent errors can result in fines and penalties that can reach millions of dollars. Accurate tracking of work and pay is also important when performing government work, where contracts usually include the ability to audit labor charges. Agencies such as the U.S. Defense Contract Audit Agency audit companies regularly to ensure they are following agreed upon processes.

Graham never realized how much was involved in tracking time and generating a paycheck, but the efforts were paying off. With the first department on its way to receiving perfect paychecks, Graham could see these changes would add up to about two and a half percent of total production payroll by the end of the year. That would save the company $5 million annually on their $200,000,000 annual payroll in operations. While they still had a long way to go to reduce unit costs by 10%, the first results were achievable quickly and would be welcome news to Spencer.

Graham wrote down the savings and forwarded to Spencer.

Operational Expense Reductions	
2.5% reduction in payroll inflation in operations	$5,000,000

In studying the details of employees' timecards and payroll, Graham did note that a significant portion of the difference between worked and paid hours was overtime. Reducing overtime was on his original list of areas to reduce unit costs, but in previous efforts, the supervisors had said overtime was necessary and any forced reductions had always negatively impacted production.

While the new timekeeping processes would eliminate some of the premium pay, there was still a significant amount of overtime being used. Graham had never guessed that he could cut payroll by almost three percent without any reduction of worked hours, so maybe it was time to look at premium pay again. This time he made a call to one of his production leads and set up a meeting two days ahead. One of the lessons Graham had learned while improving the timekeeping process was the importance of using facts to support any claim that there was waste occurring in a department, otherwise the conversations became defensive and unproductive. Generating a report showing more detail than hours worked at premium pay by department was going to be a little more difficult to put together but the company's financial analysts were pretty good and he thought it would be possible. Graham placed a call and asked the finance manager to put together a chart comparing two sets of data. The first was weekly earned hours as determined from their ERP system based on production results. The second was paid labor hours; Graham had requested that payroll hours be broken out between regular and premium hours.

CHAPTER 3

MANAGING
PREMIUM PAY

Looking over the report, Graham noticed that the earned hours (those hours that have been spent working directly on production) did not always rise and fall exactly with paid hours. This was not completely unexpected, he knew that daily disruptions, such as a broken tool, took time to fix and those did not result in earned hours. These disruptions and other hours not attributed to production were reported as labor variance. What did surprise him was that there was little correlation between earned hours and the premium hours. This surprised Graham because whenever he had asked his managers in the past why the overtime was necessary, the justification was always production related: A hot order was coming through or work was queuing up.

Graham sat down with his production manager and started looking at another report, this was overtime hours used by day of week. He noted that when looking at just premium pay over the course of several months that it was running fairly steady at 18%. He would have expected it to be more volatile since the main justification supervisors provided for using overtime was upward shifts in production volume over what was planned.

There are many types of premium pay, a shift premium for working during the night is one example, a call-in premium used to reward employees for coming in even though they are not scheduled is a second. The most common type of premium pay is overtime which is typically a 1.5 multiplier over an employee's regular wage.

As disruptions in production occur, supervisors take their most flexible resource, the workforce, and apply it to all different types of situations. The challenge in controlling the use of premium pay is that it is such a flexible technique. Premium pay such as overtime can be used to solve so many different problems that it becomes easier to use premium pay than solving the original problem. It doesn't help that employees enjoy a temporary 50% or greater increase in wages as a result. In fact they can get so used to the overtime the extra dollars become an expected part of their paycheck.

Used correctly, premium pay is a good deal for both employees and employers: employees receive an increase in pay for doing the same job they always do, and employers get a skilled resource for a very short amount of time without the additional cost of training, or incremental benefit costs.

There are also drawbacks to employers and employees. Employers offering premium pay are expecting expanded labor capacity and corresponding output in return for the extra pay. Because a supervisor might not be aware of an available employee capable of performing the work in the next department or building, the supervisor could be adding unbudgeted labor hours at a premium cost when there is already labor capacity available at regular wages.

Some companies who are hesitant to hire more full-time staff or find it difficult to hire employees with specific skills may become too dependent on overtime. For employees the over-use of premium paid hours can cause hardships. Fatigue can set in causing them to make errors. This issue is addressed around the world in many industries, one example being the Nuclear Regulatory Commission's recent introduction of NRC 10 CFR Part 26 which strictly limits the amount of overtime that can be worked by an individual. On the personal front, employees must accommodate this often last-minute request by altering their personal plans such as finding help to watch their children.

Below are some of the reasons premium pay is used. Because premium pay covers so many issues and is often used for short amounts of time per occurrence, it becomes difficult to track and manage.

- Planned premium pay to increase labor capacity for an expected increase in production.

- Unplanned premium pay to respond to an unexpected event, such as a material delay, poor performance, machine breakdown or employee absence.

- Premium pay that has become an expected part of their paycheck by employees.

- Premium pay caused by poor short or long term alignment of demand and labor capacity.

Attempts to reduce premium pay through strict overtime approval policies have limited effect. A "no overtime" policy doesn't eliminate the root cause of why premium pay is being used to begin with and only pushes the cost elsewhere such as premium freight. At the individual level, a reduction in overtime means a smaller paycheck. This makes the goal of reducing overtime an unpopular program for those benefitting from the extra pay.

Increasing approval hurdles is just a more mild form of a "no overtime" policy. Supervisors and employees learn what to say to get the overtime approved and the new approval policies only add bureaucracy and slow decision making.

What is needed to improve the management and control of premium pay is more insight as to why the premiums are being used and what other options are available that don't increase costs.

The following situations provide examples of useful and wasteful uses of premium pay.

Legitimate uses of premium pay

- Seasonality of production means the overtime hours required won't last long.

- Customer is willing to pay a premium for a rush order.

- Customer asks for extra services such as special packaging or labeling and is willing to pay a premium.

- Vacation or other planned absence coverage.

Legitimate uses of premium pay caused by other resolvable issues

- Material shortages cause production delays so the shift stays longer than planned.

- Machine break down and change-over delays result in operators staying late to catch up.

- Product quality is dropping and re-work hours increase.

- Turnover is up and the lower performance of new employees drives a need for overtime.

- More machines than usual break down during the week, causing the maintenance department to perform planned maintenance on Saturday.

- Unplanned absenteeism requires replacements to fill a shift.

- Certain skills are in short supply, requiring overtime to meet the need.

Poor use of premium pay

- Calling in an employee, when another capable and available employee is already on the premises.

- Responding to an internal or customer need through the use of premium pay when it could wait until the next day.

Intentional and un-intentional abuse of premium pay

- Slowing down work so overtime becomes required to catch up.

- Unauthorized re-prioritizing of work so overtime is required to catch up on overdue orders.

Of these 15 premium pay examples only four add expanded labor capacity to production. The rest of the examples are the result of production issues where extra labor is used to recover from a disruption. These remaining 11 uses of premium pay are opportunities to reduce operational expense without any loss to production capacity.

Managing premium pay is made more difficult because the decisions are generally made under pressure in order to resolve an immediate problem. Other options to paying someone a premium are not always evident, such as an available operator in the next department. Because there is no record kept of why the decision was made to use premium pay, there's no data that can be mined to identify root cause issues.

This is a prime opportunity for a company to reduce its labor costs while maintaining its labor capacity. But it is not a simple technology or policy fix. It is a combination of improved data and better decision making and awareness by supervisors and employees.

Fortunately most companies have the fundamentals in place to immediately begin improving the way they manage premium pay. The following example highlights how a company can reduce labor costs while maintaining high levels of service without incremental investment.

Forest City Enterprises, Inc.

Forest City Enterprises develops and manages real estate for commercial and government entities. It has a diverse workforce of 3500 employees at more than 200 sites in 25 states. Forest City's approach to controlling overtime is so complete that it can serve as a lesson to all companies.

Forest City's goal was to reduce overall overtime while maximizing its use for revenue producing activities. This meant taking a three pronged approach: improving the alignment of labor capacity to match demand, increasing decision support information and increasing awareness of an overtime reduction program throughout the company.

The first step was to make changes to the way people worked in order to provide high levels of service while eliminating "slow periods". Forest City collaborated with employees to create more flexible schedules so that as demand rises and falls, employees use regular hours rather than overtime to handle the peaks. This allows service levels to stay high while minimizing overtime. The following are some of the techniques used to accomplish this reduction:

- Staggered and rotating shifts.

- Sending people home early when work was not required.

- Alternate days off, so a weekend or holiday didn't necessarily mean overtime for all who work.

- Supervisors perform tasks during peak periods.

- Work with customers to redefine service levels.

The second step was to improve decision making when deciding if overtime should be used. In general, people try to make the best decisions they can; they understand that increased profitability leads to job security and growth. But their decisions are limited to the information available to them. Without legitimate alternatives at their fingertips, premium pay is often the fastest method to resolve an immediate problem. If there are loose controls regarding overtime, the high cost of that decision won't be realized until the end of the pay period and the specific issue causing the increase in cost will be lost in a summary report.

Finally, communicating the goals and status to employees and upper management is important to ensure that the objectives of management through the individual departments are aligned. With an increased awareness that overtime represents a significant loss of profitability, people began making better choices. Employees at Forest City Enterprises were educated that reducing labor hours is not an acceptable reason for reducing levels of service. In addition, Forest City Enterprises shared the savings with, and rewarded those that achieved their goals.

The program paid off. According to Jason Fenske, Human Resources Director for Forest City Enterprises, the efforts resulted in a 35% drop in overtime from the previous year while maintaining service levels. From a technology perspective, Forest City Enterprises used the existing data in its timekeeping system to create the new reports. This is truly a Lean success story where a rethinking of the entire way people accomplished work was considered and participation from the employees was critical to its success.

Overtime is difficult to remove from labor costs because there are often effective and ineffective uses of overtime within a company and even within a department. But this doesn't mean it should be ignored.

In addition to the techniques applied by Forest City Enterprises, here are some methods to see if premium pay is being used unnecessarily:

- Use employee schedules to track planned premium pay. Planned premium pay is generally used to address an increase in production orders or to cover for someone on vacation, both good reasons. By planning for overtime, it highlights where unplanned overtime is used, making it easier to target for reduction.

- Report on overtime compared to production output. If overtime is going up and production output isn't, there may be a production issues that needs resolution.

- Compare premium pay hours to skills. If a set of skills is in short supply, this is a good indication that additional recruiting or training efforts are required.

- Look at patterns of premium pay. If there is an intermittent use of premium pay, that's a good sign because it is likely being used to react to last minute issues. Steady levels of premium pay in a department indicate that overtime is being built into the culture rather than employees and supervisors resolving the underlying issues.

Using premium pay without a resulting expansion of production output represents opportunity to reduce labor costs. In cases that often result in the use of premium pay such as machine downtime, waiting for materials or a shortage of scheduled labor, the underlying issues must be resolved first. Otherwise their impact on the business will be translated into increased expense. In the following chapters, examples of challenging production scenarios that result in increased labor costs will be addressed.

Graham was ecstatic; after a month of efforts they were beginning to see the pay-off in getting premium pay under control. Yes, he had heard indirectly the complaints about the smaller paychecks and some employees were not happy about some of the changes to their schedules. He had responded to this with monetary rewards to individuals who attained the overtime reduction goals and educating the production teams about the changes in product pricing the company was experiencing. Overall though, premium hours were down and production had not been impacted. Raising the awareness of the program by rewarding those who had reduced hours and by posting the progress to goal had made a big difference in getting everyone to make necessary changes.

The reductions came from several places, attendance was improving, and supervisors were using overtime more judiciously to react to production issues. Awareness among employees that management was scrutinizing use of premium pay by individuals had its intended effect. Production also identified some skills that were in shortage and began cross training other employees to provide a larger pool of candidates when the regularly scheduled person wasn't available.

While the savings were significant, $9 million annually, it only amounted to 25% of the total overtime used. The challenge was that the other 75% of overtime pay was being used legitimately to increase production capacity or to resolve issues that had no other short term answer. One issue that seemed to be a recurring theme was the shortage of a particular skill on a production line. It seemed to be caused by a variety of reasons: The person originally scheduled to work had also been assigned to work on another line at the same time or the scheduler had not estimated the work correctly or one of seemingly endless reasons from individual preferences to expired certifications that caused small delays in production. As Graham thought about all the different types of issues they were solving through the use of overtime, he walked by a production supervisor's office and saw a handwritten employee schedule on the bulletin board. The number of scratch outs and different names and locations written over the original schedule suggested a hectic week. The shift had ended and employees had gone home for the day, so Graham would have to wait until tomorrow to ask the supervisor some questions.

As Graham was walking back to his office, he saw an email from Grace, the Vice President of Human Resources.

"Do you remember we started tracking safety incidents in the new system we use to track attendance? I started posting a chart highlighting the incidents on the shop floor

bulletin boards. An employee came up with an idea a couple of weeks ago to change a welding technique that would eliminate our most frequent eye incident. Since we've implemented it we've had no issues and the welders feel good about it. We called our insurance company and we will see more than two million in annual premium reductions because of this by next year."

Graham was ecstatic. This was unexpected. Even better, the savings did not come at the expense of anyone's pay or worked hours and yet the company would still save more than two million dollars a year. He sat down and started updating the calculations to see where he was towards his goal.

Operational Expense Reductions	
2.5% reduction in payroll inflation in operations	$5,000,000
Premium pay reduction	$9,000,000
Medical insurance premium reduction	$2,000,000

With these reductions in operational expense he had decreased unit costs by just over 1.5%. While Graham was proud of the achievements, he knew he had to find some bigger savings soon.

CHAPTER 4

BALANCING LABOR
AND DEMAND

"If computers could make a decent employee schedule, I'd be happy to use it."

It was obvious to Graham that the production supervisor was passionate about this subject. "But with all the data we have to enter about each person into the scheduler, which by the way changes all the time, it's just easier to manage the employee schedule by hand," the supervisor continued. "It's the same challenge we had when we cleaned up the Bill of Materials and Routings before we got a reasonable production schedule out of the ERP system. Each employee's seniority, skills, certifications, primary jobs, secondary preferences all have to be entered and maintained. Then we have to keep the swapped shifts, vacations and other planned absences up to date. And let's not even get started on the personality conflicts and car pooling issues that we have to accommodate. How can a scheduling application know all that? And even if it could, who's going to maintain all that data? We keep cutting people and yet you want us to do more, it just doesn't make sense." Visibly worked up, he continued. "To improve our flow we still have work to do on reducing the size of a production run. I know I fought it at first, but the work in process has gone down and we are able to respond to last minute orders faster because we aren't waiting weeks until an out of stock part is scheduled to run."

"In fact, think about it, because we're shrinking our production runs to become more responsive, we are performing more changeovers than ever before. If anything, our ability to schedule people is getting less predictable, not more. That's where your overtime is coming from."

And that's when the penny dropped for Graham. He realized their focus on reducing work in process and shrinking production runs had resulted in the production processes becoming agile faster than the workforce could respond. And the only way to maintain those gains in work in process and lead times was to add more labor hours, such as overtime.

In a way this was good news, the swamp was draining and now employees were becoming the constraint on the system. By focusing the company on work in process reductions and lot sizes, the company had focused on machines, materials and methods. It had not placed the same level of effort to improve its employees' ability to respond to a leaner production environment.

Graham knew the ability to respond quickly was directly related to the workforce. The machines didn't start and stop themselves and the material was handled by somebody. It was now time to start focusing their Lean production efforts on people the same way they had on materials.

The discussion with the supervisor went on the better part of the morning. Graham began to see why labor costs were actually increasing with Lean.

Before the labor cuts, supervisors were able to schedule enough people to ensure there was always some excess labor capacity in each of the departments. As production runs shortened, the numbers of changeovers increased requiring more labor. Each department was able to absorb this increase in labor demand because they were staffing to what they estimated they would need and then a little more to handle the peaks.

When the reduction in force took place last year, what management perceived as excess labor capacity was the first to go. Now when a department needed some extra labor to respond to a shift in production or it had to catch up after an issue like a material delay, supervisors tended to use overtime. So while the labor cuts last year had removed the extra hours, during those peak times when that labor was truly needed, the hours were staffed with people who were on overtime.

As Graham finished up his discussion with the supervisor he kept looking at the paper schedule. He couldn't help but think about the way other resources were managed. He could never imagine managing inventories on paper or spreadsheets again. His experience with the strategic sourcing project had taught him that lesson. Yet, here was a resource even more complex than materials and the supervisors are adamant that the only way they could manage it was on a spreadsheet printout with pencil edits. He also began to think about the number one reason the supervisor gave for sticking with paper: The data entry was harder than the scheduling process itself. But Graham realized something the supervisor hadn't. The majority of the scheduling data they needed was already sitting in a database. It had been entered as a part of the Perfect Paycheck project to ensure everyone was being paid accurately. Would it be possible to re-use that existing information to simplify the labor scheduling process?

Ideal production occurs when the four M's, Man, Machine, Material and Method, come together at just the right time. Any resource (Man, Machine, or Material) arriving early or late to an operation results in waste as one or more of the resources is idled waiting for the others. For labor, this means an individual arriving early to a particular operation represents excess labor cost. Labor arriving late creates a temporary constraint reducing the operation's throughput.

Manufacturers understand this, but getting equipment and materials together at the right time and place is tough enough, and adding employees to the mix makes it that much harder. Between employees' desire to have stable hours, the operation's requirement for specific skills and certifications, the work rules and regulations that limit what jobs can be worked, and the unpredictable personal issues that occur each day, it's no wonder that production can be tough to start on time each day.

Below is a list of the different constraints a typical scheduler must comply with to generate a viable employee schedule.

- They must make production and employee changes without breaking work rules when last minute production adjustments occur.

- They must comply with the different applicable government, state and local regulations such as meal and break laws or fatigue laws that limit the amount of time worked.

- They must comply with negotiated bargaining or workers council agreements such as rules around bumping, overtime and seniority.

- They must ensure the right mix of skills is present on the production line.

- They must staff the correct number of hours as called for by the amount and type of production.

- They must ensure the cost of the schedule is in line even though there are varying wages, premiums and overtime situations.

- They must ensure the employees needed to staff the line are available to work.

- They must ensure that employees with the right level of experience are scheduled. Too many new people can slow down a line or cause quality issues, too many senior people can exceed the labor budget.

- They must consider any special situations between employees such as a personality conflict.

This list contains two types of challenges for schedulers. The first is aligning the labor supply and demand while staying within cost targets. The second is the scheduling rules that must be followed to ensure compliance with government, union and company policies and regulation. These two challenges are compounded by the pressure of time to create and update schedules throughout the week.

While significant focus has been placed on managing materials and machines, it has generally been left to department supervisors to manage the variability within the workforce. The result is that labor scheduling expertise is held by a few people who create them regularly. These people are often stressed because all of these constraints can only be met once demand is firmed up. With demand becoming more volatile as companies move from push to pull, labor scheduling is only getting more difficult due to increasing variability.

Variability forcing change to a labor schedule has two different sources. The first is the fluctuations in work and comes from a variety of causes. It can range from customers changing their minds about delivery dates and order sizes, machines breaking down and poor quality materials to environmental conditions causing production to run slower than expected.

The second source of variability is caused by the individuals on the schedule. Turnover and retirement of employees affect the mix of the employee demographic. Training, absenteeism, vacations and personal issues also ensure that a steady employee schedule is rare.

There are techniques to automate and simplify labor scheduling. But rather than focus on improving the ability to deal with all the daily issues that arise, the first step should be looking at ways to remove the employee based causes of that variability.

To start, employee variability can be broken down into three categories:

- Predictable employee variability that can be planned for well in advance such as trends (turnover and retirement) and individual events (vacations or expired certifications).

- Daily unplanned employee variability that can be controlled such as attendance.

- Daily unplanned issues that cannot be controlled or predicted such as someone's child waking up ill in the morning.

Many supervisors manage these different types of variability the same way. They have a week's notice or less and then react to the problem with their own methods of problem solving. The most common solutions to an employee driven scheduling problem are:

- Temporarily ignore the issue until it can be resolved, such as an expired certification.

- Keep operators on the job busy by producing something other than what was planned and put it into inventory if it's not needed.

- Slow down or delay production until the right resources are found, resulting in the problem moving downstream (if there is no disruption it's an indication they were overstaffed to begin with).

- Use overtime or other premium pay to expand labor capacity to resolve the issue.

- Have supervisors step in and perform the work themselves if possible.

- Find someone else onsite available and capable of doing the job.

Of all these techniques, the best of a bad situation is to find an under-utilized resource onsite. A supervisor stepping in to perform the work occasionally is not the worst case, but presumably they were hired to perform another job at a higher wage so in effect this technique becomes a form of premium pay with respect to the job.

If these techniques are used regularly to manage daily variability, this is evidence that there is significant variability within the workforce and it's affecting production. By thinking about the problem in a Lean context, the techniques in "Single Minute Exchange of Dies" (SMED) can be applied. This method has been developed to speed the process of equipment changeover to increase flexibility in production and utilization of equipment. While there are several techniques within SMED that can be applied to labor scheduling, two will be described here: converting internal processes to external processes and mechanization.

Converting Internal Processes Into External Processes

"Internal process" means those activities that can occur only while the machine is stopped. "External process" means things that can be accomplished whether the machine is running or not. The idea is to perform as much work preparing for a changeover before the machine stops so that its downtime is reduced during the actual changeover. This type of work might be tactical change such as kitting all the tools required or a strategic change such as redesigning stamping dies so less adjustment is required once they are installed into the machine.

With respect to employee scheduling, any scheduling change the supervisor must deal with on a specific day of production can be considered an internal process, for example, a delay because someone hasn't been trained or certified on a specific operation should never be dealt with on the day of production. Anything supervisors can resolve beforehand should be actively managed as an external process. So while the workforce remains highly variable, much of this variability is foreseeable and some of it is controllable. By resolving the problems before production is scheduled to start, production will be subject to less delay.

Moving internal labor processes to external processes will require help from other departments, most notably Human Resources. Changing labor processes cannot be accomplished by production supervisors alone. Demographic analysis, recruiting and training are complementary efforts that will be required to enact these changes.

The following areas outline several characteristics of workforce variability that are predictable and can be managed long before a schedule is created. Often these issues are left un-addressed and managed on a one-off basis by the employee's supervisor. As a result, the work that these employees were expected to perform must be re-assigned with little warning or planning. This makes the following areas good candidates for moving from an internal process to an external process. For those companies that have begun work on achieving the Perfect Paycheck, most if not all of this data required to create or improve external processes is already available within their workforce management system.

Employee Turnover

While some turnover can be good because wages are moderated and new ideas are introduced as new employees share their experiences, there is a point at which turnover becomes a drag on performance. Labor scheduling with high levels of turnover is difficult. The reasons for turnover are varied. It could be the way shifts are designed or a job that needs to be re-evaluated to make it less stressful. It might also be the way a supervisor interacts with his employees. It can be difficult to decide what level of turnover is too much because measuring the financial impact of turnover on operations isn't easy.

This was the exact challenge faced by a contract cosmetic manufacturer. A finance led labor strategy to control costs and improve production flexibility included hiring all temporary labor for production operators. But the challenge of meeting production goals with what was effectively a new staff each day was increasing supervisor turnover and new supervisors were not as effective at mustering the staff and getting the lines started in the morning. A frustrated Operations VP recognized the problem, but didn't have the data to support the cause-and-effect relation of decline in productivity with the increase in supervisor turnover. Unfortunately, he was not able to make his case and unable to effect the changes at the company he knew were required. As a result, he left the company to focus his efforts elsewhere.

Understanding the causes of turnover can help human resources and management either resolve the underlying issues or recruit more actively to ensure there is a steady supply of new hires that are trained and productive when needed.

Employee Retirement

Retirement is also becoming an increasingly important factor that has to be built into workforce planning. It may take more hours for a new hire to get the same job done as an experienced worker. And if there is a significant wave of retirement, lines can slow or quality can deteriorate as undocumented knowledge of techniques is lost. Workforce planning can look at employee tenure and age and forecast the rate of retirement in specific jobs. Training budgets and labor standards can then be adjusted appropriately in advance versus hiring employees back as contractors at a higher cost.

Skills and Overtime

Look at overtime by skill or position. Are there some skills or positions that are consistently difficult to fill in the schedule? Make better hiring choices by using facts to identify the specific skills and shifts required rather than adding to the general labor budget. An apprentice program is another option when external talent is not available for immediate hire. Often welders fall into this camp. From ship building to rail car fabrication, companies differentiate their product based on welding techniques. They find that it is hard to hire employees with the right skills when they are needed. Internal training is a good way to provide a career path and ensure a steady supply of talent.

Labor Utilization, Performance, Quality and Absenteeism

Using labor standards (a defined amount of time that a specific operation should take) as the only metric to staff for the upcoming year is only going to lead to continued challenges. Even when labor standards are accurate, if labor utilization and quality levels are not factored into the labor budget, variances will continue to occur as more labor is required than was originally planned. It's better to have a difficult discussion about the actual labor utilization, performance and quality requirements when building the budget than to push the problem of an understaffed budget to the supervisors on a weekly basis.

Understanding all the labor hours required to produce a product, not just what is calculated from the ideal scenario documented in the production process is necessary to budget next year's labor accurately. This means understanding actual labor effectiveness. A technique to measure labor effectiveness will be introduced in the next chapter.

Vacations and Leave of Absence

If requests are still being made with paper forms, there is a high probability that not everyone who will be absent is being accounted for by the labor schedule. As a part of delivering the Perfect Paycheck, accurate time off records are a necessity and these planned vacations, shift swaps and other absences should be populated on the employee schedule automatically. This provides the supervisors with time to react before production is ready to begin.

Attendance

This is an example of an unforeseeable event that is controllable. One of the most common issues that affect attendance is the fair and equitable enforcement of the policy. Many companies have found that supervisors have a difficult time enforcing attendance policies because it is hard for them to confront employees. It could be they are friends or they know of a personal situation that is causing attendance issues or the regularly tardy employee is otherwise a star performer. By automating the enforcement of the policy, this slippage caused by the human tendencies of supervisors is removed. As a result, individuals will realize that attendance is not an area where there is a gray area and on time arrival will improve. Careful consideration should be given to the attendance policy to ensure there is a balance and that good behavior is also rewarded.

Mechanization

Mechanization is the process of automating repetitive processes. When applied to labor scheduling, mechanizing repetitive process reduces the time and cost required to make changes, eliminates mistakes and shortens the learning curve for new schedulers. The following are several scheduling processes that are good candidates for mechanizing. Mechanizing also provides another advantage, because decision making processes are accelerated, the process becomes more agile.

Unplanned Issues on the Day of Production

Even the best laid plans are subject to change. This could be an employee driven change or simply a change in production plans. If someone "calls off" (calls and lets the supervisor know they won't be in today), the supervisor has a number of options as discussed in the previous chapter. By mechanizing or automating the decision making process, the method and outcome becomes standardized across all supervisors and speeds up finding the best answer to the problem. For example, if it would take 20 minutes to walk or call the other department supervisors to locate someone, a supervisor might opt to use overtime and ask someone to stay late. By using an electronic scheduling assistant to review the employees currently on site the process could be reduced to a few minutes.

Mechanizing Repetitive Tasks

Many of the rules that constrain a scheduler can be documented and automated. A specific set of skills required to staff a production line or the seniority of individual when making a substitution are both examples of company and union or workers council agreements. Minimum time between shifts or a specific certification to operate a piece of equipment is an example of a regulation that applies to a schedule. Automating either the population of the shifts or at least checking manual schedule edits against policies and regulations eliminates mistakes and speeds up the process of creating and editing a schedule. It also makes creating and editing a schedule more accessible for people without years of experience.

Accommodating Demand Changes

While there is increasingly less control of the workload influencing a production schedule, as a company moves from forecasted production to customer driven, one method of improving a scheduler's efficiency is to ensure production demand is accurately translated into labor workload. Supervisors that make manual labor adjustments as production requirements change are prone to over and under-scheduling labor. Automating the process to determine the correct number and type of operators required is a three step process.

First, identify the production drivers that cause the number of employees required to fluctuate. For a food processor, it could be quantity and quality of the harvest. Another variable to when employees are needed could vary based on the transportation time from the field to the processing plant.

The second step is to calculate the labor standards that translate production demand into labor required by individual role. If there are three different types of jobs and 20 people on a production line there will be up to three different labor standards for each demand driver.

The third step is to create the rules that determine how a schedule is created. For example, if there is double the usual amount of materials, should the line be staffed to twice the usual number of people or should the duration of the production run be doubled? The answer to this is dependent on the capacity of the production line or a machine. If the production line is running at capacity, adding more people won't help; the schedule will have to be extended in time to process the extra materials.

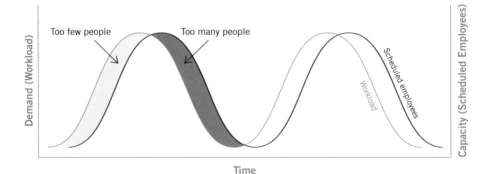

Losses in scheduling occur in two ways. When companies under-schedule, orders are delayed and overtime increases. A second way is when companies over-schedule labor either because they don't have an accurate method to translate demand to labor or they are compensating for unplanned shortages in labor.

With these three steps completed a workload generator, which is a piece of software, can be used to take the information on drivers, standards, and production constraints and create a schedule template that has the right number and types of jobs for the production line based on what needs to be produced. At this point there are only job titles in the schedule. No specific people have been assigned to the schedule yet.

Mechanizing the Process of Populating a Shift with Specific Employees

With a specific shift's schedule ready to be populated with the individuals, there are still a number of constraints that limit the qualified individuals that can be assigned. Constraints include employee availability based on vacations and work preferences, work rules such as minimum time between shifts, lowest possible cost or seniority ranking and job specific requirements such as skill and certification requirements.

The challenge for schedulers is that each time a change in the schedule takes place they must make adjustments to all the people affected. As the pace of production speeds up in an agile environment, people begin to take shortcuts. They rely on their memory and will make the best decisions they can under the circumstances. This results in production lines that are over and under staffed and compliance issues when rules are broken.

An employee scheduling engine automating this process can often populate 80% or more of the jobs with specific employees in minutes. It's then up to the scheduler to manually fill in the remaining open positions and make adjustments for those soft preferences that can't be captured within the rules. The benefit to a supervisor or scheduler is that it can reduce several hours of work to 20 minutes. Even more beneficial is that during the day of production when a change needs to be made, the scheduler can click a button and get the system to make its recommendations on the change in seconds.

National Frozen Foods is a great example of a food processor that has applied these Lean scheduling techniques with success at their processing plants. Next we'll take a look at exactly how they have done it.

National Frozen Foods Corporation

National harvests, freezes and then packages peas, corn, green beans, lima beans, squash and carrots for customers in North America and Asia. Its operations are seasonal, requiring 600 people throughout the year for blending and packaging the vegetables based on customer orders. During harvest time an additional 700 temporary employees are hired.

Throughout the harvest, field supervisors drive to the fields which are located 30 minutes to several hours from one of four processing plants. At the end of the day they return with a plan detailing which fields are ready for harvest. Schedulers working from a standard schedule then fine tune that schedule to assure the right number of combine drivers, field workers and truck drivers based on the type of vegetable, size of the field and location from the plant. They also begin scheduling which production lines to use and how they should be staffed.

Staffing a production line consists of a baseline of specific people who have certain skills and seniority and then adding other operators based on the fluctuations of the harvest and crop.

In the morning as the field department begins harvesting, supervisors develop a good sense of the yield and quality of the crop and an estimate of when the product should reach the plant. They phone in this information to the schedulers who then fine tune the schedule to accommodate the changes in volume, time and the actual effort required to clean and sort the vegetables as they begin processing.

At the same time, the schedulers also schedule the packaging lines to handle the ongoing customer orders.

Business Analyst Michele Cyrus, who oversees National Frozen Food's scheduling project, noted that a scheduler position requires working 10 hours a day, seven days a week during harvest time. Schedulers face many challenges during harvest. Time is of the essence once the vegetables are picked. Sugars begin converting to starch, degrading their quality. A production line that is not ready to start processing when the crop arrives can cause deterioration in quality of the product. Additionally, there are the personnel issues to address. Some employees will not work on the same line together. Others can only work the same shifts because they car pool to work together. As a result of these challenges, double scheduling, which is when one person is assigned to two lines simultaneously, can occur, resulting in one processing line missing a person.

National may also hire over 100 temporary employees in one day during harvest season. As one of their union agreements, National is required to schedule a job based on seniority. But with dozens of people hired on the same day, National needed a process to determine the seniority of a person based on more than just the hire date. Different plants settled on different methods, one used alphabetic order of the last name, others assigned seniority by the order new employees arrived at orientation. But using these seniority lists manually was difficult.

To automate the scheduling process National began implementing electronic labor schedules. This included scheduling templates and an automated scheduling assistant to augment its manual scheduling efforts. The scheduling templates were created for each combination of volume and quality of each type of harvest. Based on what is planned the scheduler selects the appropriate template. Using the scheduling assistant, the scheduler simply selects the open job and the scheduling assistant automatically fills in the job with the person who is most qualified while conforming to the seniority rules, certification and skill requirements and other union rules.

In addition to eliminating the double scheduling of certain people and seniority based grievances, there are several other benefits:

- Overtime for the scheduler is reduced.

- The level of effort from the payroll employees is reduced and pay is accurate. National pays different rates for different jobs. Previously when the job transfers were manually collected, payroll clerks had to track down any missing details and handle any employee questions about pay. With automatic tracking of job transfers, the process of calculating different job rates during a pay period is simplified and accurate.

- One of the most interesting benefits occurred when the son of one of the schedulers had the opportunity to participate in Little League Play Off's in another city during a harvest. With the electronic scheduling tools in place, the scheduler was able to attend! Because the information was completely electronic, the scheduler was able to create the schedules remotely, only requiring internet access and a phone to communicate with the field supervisors.

Flexing the Workforce

Even with the perfect schedule, changing weather, unplanned absenteeism, and last minute customer orders all work to drag down productivity and increase unit labor costs. There are also longer term issues such as seasonality and upturns and downturns in the business. As a result often there is too much labor, too little labor or the skill mix is wrong. To ensure that the right amount of labor capacity is available for the amount of work required manufacturers have employed a number of techniques to make small and large adjustments to their workforce.

- Cross training employees to substitute for each other.

- Calling in employees who weren't scheduled or keeping them from an earlier shift.

- Sending employees home early.

- Hiring temporary labor.

- Forcing employees to use accrued time off during slow periods.

- Investing down time in cleaning, training and continuous improvement.

- Voluntary lay-offs and furloughs.

- Forced lay-offs.

A flexible workforce provides several benefits in addition to improving labor utilization and controlling costs. The learning curve for some skills can take months or years to build. Laying-off and re-hiring people as business demand changes can drain the talent pool at a company. Additionally employees need stability to provide for themselves and their families. A company that treats its employees without respect to their personal needs will not receive the same innovations and effort as those companies that provide a more stable environment.

Graham reflected on the past several months after introducing the automated scheduling processes. In the beginning the supervisors were resistant to leave their paper schedules. They felt it was the one area of control they had in dealing with the daily fluctuations of the business. This mindset had slowly changed as the issues such as shortages of certain skill sets were teased out of the process, reducing the amount of last minute change a supervisor had to deal with. Identifying and solving the labor scheduling issues often meant gathering people from multiple departments and all had to agree on changes that would seem to benefit others.

Supervisors were reluctant to identify idle employees. They were concerned that their employee's downtime would reflect poorly on them. Secondly the supervisors worried that this idle time would be eliminated from their labor budgets and therefore reduce their ability to provide surge capacity. This behavior only began changing when Graham relaxed metrics that encouraged supervisors to optimize their own performance regardless of the impact to others.

In some cases new pay policies were written as people began performing work in new ways. For example, with people transferring across a wider variety of departments, new pay policies had to be set up to ensure labor charges were accurately tracked. The need for this arose when supervisors were unsure where to charge overtime when their employees worked over forty hours but had spent the middle of the week working in a different department.

The unions, well aware of the pressure to relocate the plants overseas, warily agreed to some changes that allowed employees to change jobs and flex their hours without the large premiums they had previously demanded.

With attendance improving and department supervisors agreeing to transfer employees to accommodate surges in one department, everyone felt more comfortable scheduling only the resources required for the planned work.

While Graham started the scheduling analysis focused on reducing overtime, he realized he had also actually reduced hidden labor buffers in the schedule. As a result, not only had overtime decreased by another 10%, but the overstaffing to accommodate shortages was down and grievances based on seniority and bumping issues had all but vanished.

Supervisors were finally willing to relinquish their paper schedules. The electronic schedules were connected to the timekeeping system and supervisors quickly realized that their data entry concerns were unfounded. They also recognized the benefit of keeping the schedules up to date each day. When everyone had access to current data, they would have a better chance of solving their own labor issues without increasing labor costs.

While no one had expected the accountants to benefit from these changes, the increased tracking of employee transfers and reductions in premium pay had started to shrink the unexplained labor variances. There were still challenges to be addressed, but Graham noticed in his monthly variance meetings that the accountants were becoming much more targeted in their questions. Production managers didn't feel as though they had to justify the way they ran their departments. The facts were there for all to see and variances could be rationally discussed.

Payroll administrators had also commented on the changes. They were receiving fewer complaints about paycheck errors. This reduced the time required to review the paper schedules and interview supervisors about who worked where each pay period.

These scheduling improvements took out the "just in case" labor, reduced premium pay and eliminated many of the grievances that took both time and money to process. In total, they had eliminated another $12 million in cost.

But even with this progress, Graham had not reached his goal. In just over six months, the team had cut $23 million out of operational expense. Unit costs were now down 2.4%. While these were the biggest improvements the company had ever seen in such a short time, it was still not enough to meet the target of 10%. And at this point he wasn't sure how else he was going to be able to reduce labor hours.

Graham went back to his office and added the scheduling savings to his records.

Operational Expense Reductions	
2.5% reduction in payroll inflation in operations	$5,000,000
Premium pay reduction	$9,000,000
Medical insurance premium reduction	$2,000,000
Improved labor scheduling	$12,000,000

Graham took out the paper that held his unit cost formula and reviewed the ideas that had been submitted. The sheet of paper was getting fairly well marked up at this point. But all the notes were on the top half of the equation, the expense half. Graham considered the idea about increasing throughput at the bottleneck operations in the plant. He had participated in a number of projects in the past where significant gains had already been made reducing lot size and increasing machine throughput. What stuck in his mind was how convinced his production supervisor was that these gains were actually requiring more labor. They had always measured progress in terms of inventory, cycle time and throughput. There had never been an effort to analyze the impact on labor. The reductions in lead time and the increases in throughput were always large enough that a small increase in labor could be justified. Would it be possible to improve throughput with even less labor?

But penciling in a higher production volume to reduce unit costs was a long way from making it happen on a daily basis in the plant. Graham packed up for the night and considered how he might answer that question.

CHAPTER 5

USING LABOR INFORMATION TO MAKE OPERATIONAL DECISIONS

▊▊▊▊

Graham walked into the plant mid-morning. It was easily the size of a football field. Even though it was well lit you couldn't see the opposite wall because of the tool cribs and other enclosed areas. Over the past three years, they had re-organized much of the equipment to improve production flow. Receiving was at one end of the plant and shipping was on the other end. As Graham walked through, he could see the transition from raw materials to finished products. He stopped at a production cell, notorious for having production challenges. These challenges were legitimate; this cell performed one of the more complicated operations. The step that caused the most trouble was an operation that pressed a steel rod into a steel cylinder. The operation was a result of a number of previous cost reduction ideas over the years that had significantly reduced the machining costs of the final assembly but had required what was previously a single part to be machined as two individual parts and then attached to each other. The idea to re-attach the two parts without any fasteners was a stroke of genius by one of the manufacturing engineers. The only problem was that the cylinder had to be heated and then the rod slowly pressed in two inches with extremely low tolerances in both axial alignment and depth of insertion. Because the machined surfaces of each part were complex and delicate, the fixtures that held onto the pieces during the heating and pressing operation were sensitive to positioning by the operators.

The lay-offs last year had caused some friction with the unions and that friction was still felt today. As he approached the production lead, Graham could tell right away this wasn't going to be an easy discussion. Graham decided to change tactics, this conversation might go better in a group. He recognized two of the production operators who he had been able to help out of tough spots in the past. He asked the production lead if they could all meet at lunch. Graham offered to buy lunch for everyone which was appreciated.

When they met later for lunch, he started off the meeting by asking about the changes they had made over the last couple of years as a result of the Lean programs.

The team was happy to comply. "We've applied 5S to our work areas. It's helped us put away the tools we don't use too often and keep the ones we need all the time right by each of our stations. It only saves a couple of seconds each time we use them but that adds up.

"We've been trained to fix our own equipment if it's something small. This way we don't have to wait for maintenance."

The production lead couldn't resist chiming in. "I started measuring the Overall Equipment Effectiveness of the press. One of the areas we improved was the heating and pressure profiles of the press. Making the ramp ups a little gentler reduced our scrap rate by eight percent."

Once they got rolling, the group had rattled off another five improvements they had made over the years.

Graham noticed that many of the improvements were focused on issues the production operators could control and they were even taking on more work such as the machine adjustments to further increase their control of the process. He congratulated them on their success and asked another question. "If you could make the other operations and departments, including engineering and purchasing, do whatever they could to help you perform better, what should they do?"

"Oh that's a long list." They laughed.

"I'm listening."

The team went on. "The upstream operations could let us know how long their delays will be. We never know if it will be one hour or four hours. If we knew it was going to be four hours in the beginning, we could fit in a changeover and a different job. As it is, we think it's going to be an hour and then we end up waiting four. They say it's not their fault because they were told by the crane operator that it would only be a little while to move the assemblies but then it took hours.

"We learned how to adjust the equipment ourselves because maintenance is always in such a rush to get here, fix the problem and leave, but they don't take the time to do it right and the machine goes out of adjustment too fast. They need to figure out a way to keep this machine in specification longer."

"Purchasing needs to stop buying such cheap steel. We complained to the engineers *that sometimes it cracks during the pressing operation. We get blamed for not aligning it correctly, but we know it's the lead stringers in the material that the engineers are approving to keep the material costs down.*

Graham had seen this happen many times. Other departments were optimizing their processes; purchasing was reducing material costs, and maintenance was focused on reducing the downtime of the equipment per event. While these efforts improved their metrics, they really just passed the buck into the production processes. His department then looked like they were increasing the scrap rate or taking longer to perform their jobs when really they were feeling the effects of the problems introduced by other departments.

He also knew his people weren't perfect either. Sometimes they took it a little easy and then rushed to catch up and scrap rates would increase.

The challenge in eliminating these problems had been identifying the root cause of the problem. For example, Graham knew if the operators were careful about aligning the two components, even the so called "bad material" performed fine. When the manufacturing engineers worked at the production cell with the operators, they couldn't re-create the cracking in the cylinder. A couple of days after the engineers left, the cracking started to appear again.

With the increase in operators transferring to different jobs to improve production flexibility and labor utilization, it was no longer as easy to point to one person if a problem cropped up.

Graham thought about the benefits payroll and accounting received when production improved their tracking of operators as they transferred departments throughout the day: Reduced unexplained labor variances and more accurate pay. He remembered the consultant saying that you could find waste in the process caused by materials and machines by focusing on what labor was doing to compensate. Graham wondered if he extended his tracking of people by not only what department they were in, but also what they were working on, could they identify even more waste originating from other resources and processes?

All manufacturers have the same goal: to efficiently process raw materials into finished products at the rate of customer demand. While the goal is simple, it is difficult to achieve. If unused raw materials are degrading by the day or have a high carrying cost, the manufacturer needs to identify other products that can absorb those materials or temporarily increase customer demand by selling at a lower price. If customer demand is higher than current production capacity, production needs to temporarily increase its rate of production.

There are many examples of production disruptions; raw materials arrive late, or are of a size, quality or quantity not expected, machines break down, tooling wears, individuals don't show up to work on time and customers make last minute changes to their orders. Additionally, many of the problems don't disappear at the end of a shift, they just remain for the next shift.

As an issue is resolved, the delay it causes requires extra resources to catch up. In production a second machine or production line is activated if available, employees are asked to stay late and earn premium pay, and extra materials are kept on hand in case raw material shipments are late. If production can't make up enough time, premium freight is used to deliver the order on time. Each of these is an example of the methods production managers use to handle disruptions but result in increased costs.

Rather than resign themselves to the extra cost of increasing and decreasing capacity based on daily production issues, practitioners of the Toyota Production System (TPS) have evolved many tools and concepts to empower their employees to find ways to adapt to production fluctuations without adding cost.

Many of these concepts and tools evolved around understanding and "seeing" the entire process rather than sequentially focusing improvement efforts on one operation after another. A TPS practitioner's philosophy is the faster an issue is identified and addressed, the smaller the impact on production. By understanding the entire process, individuals making decisions at one operation are cognizant of the impact that decision will have on others.

These tools and concepts have been developed to assist in optimizing the performance of the four M's, Man, Materials, Machines and Methods. For Methods, the concept of standard work was created. TPS found that the more well known and repeatable the process, the better employees became at reproducing it. Standardized work is comprised of three elements:

- Takt time - The rate at which products must be made to meet customer demand.

- Work sequence - The specific set of operations an operator performs within takt time.

- Standard inventory - The amount of inventory required to keep a process operating smoothly.

This approach to repeatable processes resulted in improved quality and efficiency.

For Materials, the concept of kan-ban was introduced. Commonly used by manufacturers and other material intensive industries, it is a visual signaling system that alerts employees that inventory is getting low and it should be re-ordered. This ensures that production doesn't stop because it has run out of raw materials. It also provides a simple mechanism to manage inventory so purchasing and operations, out of fear of starving a production line, do not stockpile too much inventory resulting in excess costs. A common example of kan-ban is used in the grocery store. A tag on the magazine rack lets employees know they should re-order a specific magazine. The tag includes the ordering details to ensure the employees have all the information they need to re-order the correct magazine.

Toyota Production System's Six Major Machine Losses

For Machines, the concept of the six major machine losses was created. Its genesis was in the fact that it is very expensive to add production capacity by purchasing equipment. Additionally an equipment purchase generally represents a large increment in capacity when often only a small increment is required. As Toyota was developing TPS, they found that when the actual output of an existing piece of equipment was measured, it was often significantly lower than the theoretical output stated on its "name plate". The realization that there is additional capacity within existing equipment led to identify the issues that reduced production capacity. This research led to the creation of the six major machine losses. By focusing on these losses, a manufacturer can identify what is causing the difference between the theoretical output of their equipment and the actual output production is experiencing.

Many people in production are familiar with the metric that takes the cumulative effect of these six major losses described in the three categories of Availability, Performance and Quality. This compound metric defined by the mathematical product of these three categories is known as Overall Equipment Effectiveness (OEE) and it highlights the interdependence of the three individual key performance indicators (KPI), Availability, Performance and Quality. For example, Availability, Performance and Quality may all be running at 87%, 95% and 99% respectively, but because the machine is only producing parts when it's running and only as many parts as performance allows and the only saleable parts are those that meet the quality standard... the real output of the machine is the product of the individual key performance indicators:

OEE = Availability x Performance x Quality

Or in our example:

OEE = 87% x 95% x 99% = 82%

In other words, even though each individual metric looks pretty good, the cumulative effect of all those losses means the machine is actually only producing 82 saleable parts when its ideal capability is 100.

The image below illustrates how the losses accumulate due to the interdependence of the individual metrics.

The following chart provides examples of where the six major losses occur.

OEE Category	Major Loss Category	Example of Loss
Availability Availability is the ratio of time the machine is actually running divided by the amount of time the machine was scheduled to be running.	Breakdown	• Tooling failures • Unplanned maintenance • Unplanned operator absence • Equipment failure
	Changeover	• Set-up/Changeover • Material shortages • Set-up personnel shortages • Major adjustments • Warm-up time
Performance Performance is the ratio of the actual output of the machine divided by the expected output (or machine standard).	Reduced speed	• Poor quality material • Under nameplate capacity • Equipment wear • Operator inefficiency
	Small stops	• Jams • Misfeeds • Sensor blocked • Cleaning/Checking
Quality Quality has many definitions, but a common one is the ratio of saleable parts produced divided by the total parts made.	Scrap or rework	• Operator error • Tooling wear • Material out of spec
	Yield or start-up losses	• Incomplete set-up • Operator error

Managing the Final M – Overall Labor Effectiveness™ (OLE)

When it comes to managing the final M, Man, there are no comparable Lean methodologies to measure and manage labor losses. While there are plenty of individual labor metrics, they don't achieve TPS's objective of seeing the entire process and highlighting the interdependency of different functions within the process.

It's not completely surprising though, because measuring people is difficult. As the most flexible resource, individuals are expected to perform a wide variety of duties and react to many situations. Mark Nguyen, Project Manager, from Ceradyne Incorporated comments "You can put a product on the table and the next day you have a fairly high certainty that it will be in the same place, have the same properties and be in the same condition as it was the day before. The same cannot be said about the workforce. Each day it's different."

It can be argued that the labor losses are embedded in the other metrics that measure the performance of materials or machines. While this is true, the details contained in these metrics don't include enough information to identify specific labor losses. For example, the OEE metric is often taken directly from a machine. But when looking for the root cause of a performance issue, it would be difficult to identify that machine performance was reduced because the operator had been working too much overtime recently and was tired.

There are also situations where there is no machine involved in an individual operation. One example is a team of welders installing valves on a rail car. If this operation is the bottleneck in production, it's important to understand where losses are occurring so they can be eliminated and capacity increased. Where is the data feeding the calculation of the OEE metric to be sourced?

Similar to the six major losses for a Machine, these losses also apply to Man. Examples of these losses are detailed in the figure later in the chapter and are organized into the same categories, Availability, Performance and Quality. Just as the metric of OEE calculates the effectiveness of a machine at a particular operation, a metric called Overall Labor Effectiveness™ (OLE™) is used to calculate the effectiveness of labor at an operation.

OLE = Availability x Performance x Quality

When labor and machines are working together at a particular operation, the value of OEE and OLE will always be the same. The difference in the metrics becomes apparent when an attempt is made at reducing the losses and identifying root cause issues. While OEE will be driven by detailed information available from the machine, it will have significantly less information about the labor such as who was originally scheduled, who actually tended the machine, operator skills, tenure and applicable pay rules. OEE has no visibility into the indirect staff that supports the operation such as material handlers, maintenance mechanics and changeover technicians. These people all have an impact on losses. The OLE metric complements OEE and has detailed information about all the different individuals operating and supporting the operation.

In addition to the shortfalls in labor details, Overall Equipment Effectiveness doesn't address another critical component of production, the actual cost of labor at the operation. Labor costs can vary based on the wages or premiums paid to the operators. Ignoring the impact of labor cost can leak profits because there are several ways to improve OEE scores by increasing labor costs. For example, to increase the performance component of OEE, a supervisor might always schedule the most senior people to an operation that's under scrutiny. Or to improve the utilization component, the amount of time a maintenance person spends on the equipment might be increased beyond what was budgeted.

The following table provides examples of the labor information tracked by Overall Labor Effectiveness organized by its major categories.

OLE Category	Major Loss Category	Example of Loss
Availability Availability is the ratio of time the operators are working productively divided by the amount of time the operators were scheduled.	Breakdown	• Lack of training and experience • Unplanned absenteeism • Maintenance mechanics delayed • Poorly scheduled breaks and lunches • Material handlers starved the machine
	Changeover	• Set-up personnel shortages or delays • Lack of training, skills and experience
Performance Performance is the ratio of the actual output of the operators divided by the expected output (or labor standard).	Reduced speed	• Operator inefficiency due to lack of skills, experience or training
	Small stops	• Poor operator technique due to lack of skills, experience or training
Quality Quality has many definitions, but a common one is the ratio of saleable parts divided by the total parts produced.	Scrap or rework	• Operator error • Set-up team error • Maintenance mechanic error
	Yield or start-up losses	• Set-up team error • Maintenance mechanic error • Operator error

Examples of labor losses at an operation that would be difficult to diagnose using the OEE metric.

Using Labor Information To Make
Operational Decisions

The reason OEE and OLE are complementary is they begin as identical metrics; they measure the same individual key performance indicators of Availability, Performance and Quality in an operation. By measuring both, the historical details and interdependence of the machine, the materials and the labor can be made available and reconciled. To deliver this labor detail without OLE requires manual efforts to track down the schedules, costs, skills, tenure and performance of the individual operators, maintenance mechanics, set up technicians and materials handlers, as well as the supervisors. Who has the time to do this? As a result it's not done and assumptions about labor related losses are made or go unresolved.

This granular labor data already exists in the human resources, timekeeping and scheduling systems. For most manufacturers, the challenge is reconciling exactly who worked on a machine for what specific period of time as well as what they did when they were not actively operating the machine. This 100% reconciliation of productive and unproductive labor hours to production and equipment hours is where workforce management systems bring together the details of the workforce with the other 3M's; Methods, Materials and Machines. By knowing where every labor hour is spent, attaching a name to that labor hour and what was accomplished with that time, significantly better decisions can be made about how to use it in the future and where waste can be eliminated in an operation.

Graham started asking more questions about the press operation. Now that they were measuring OEE what information did they have? The supervisor told him that availability was measured off the machine. And that cycle time was also measured, but that they actually calculated the OEE metric in a spreadsheet since they had to get the machine standard (the amount of time it takes a machine to complete a cycle) from the ERP system. The quality results were entered manually at the end of each shift. Along with that data, the machine itself provided additional information such as operating mode (run, off, standby), cycle time, operating temperature, and pressure as examples. At the end of each shift the score was calculated and the supervisors could discuss issues and opportunities during the shift change.

Graham looked at the history of the OEE metrics and also the underlying individual KPI's of Availability, Performance and Quality. Each of the KPI's varied over the different shifts, but he didn't see any specific trends.

He asked the production lead what he thought the biggest issues were. The production lead acknowledged that after the gains from changing the pressure and temperature variables, there wasn't any pattern that he could see.

But Graham knew this operation had significant quality and performance issues. As he dug into the details of the spreadsheet there were no visible patterns or obvious causes of the problems. He also called the production manager over to get his thoughts.

"Can you give me a list of the people who worked on this operation for the past two months as well the list of the maintenance mechanics and set up technicians who touched this machine?" Graham asked.

"We can get the people who worked in this department and who was scheduled for maintenance and set-up. That new system will let us pull those names pretty quickly but we've only been using it for a month so I'll have to look at the paper schedules for the rest. In either case I'll still have to track down who actually worked on this piece of equipment. I should be able to look through the list and circle most of those people for you. Can you give me a couple of days?" replied the production manager.

One common method used for continuous improvement was described in Chapter 4, the Single Minute Exchange of Dies (SMED). As described in that chapter, one of the techniques in this method is to separate internal and external activities. Internal activities are those efforts only possible when the process is stopped. External activities are those activities that can be executed while the process is operating. For example, does a die need reconditioning or a motor need to be rebuilt while the machine is down or can a spare be ready for immediate replacement and the rebuilding and reconditioning processes take place as a separate external process?

By analyzing the following processes, individuals focused on improving the effectiveness of operations will realize they need to understand how people from a number of different departments are interacting with the operation and if the activities contained within those processes are internal or external to the operation in question.

- Set-up

- Maintenance

- Material handling

- Machine operation

- Quality control

This is where OLE and its detailed labor data complement OEE. To understand all the variables impacting a specific activity, an organization not tracking labor at an operational level must manually collect the labor details from a variety of paper and electronic sources. Some of the details might not be captured anywhere. Because manually collecting this data is a time consuming and challenging exercise, a limited set of data is collected. This problem is compounded when the team is analyzing more than one piece of equipment over an extended period of time.

By tracking OLE, the workforce management system can track the entire workforce, both those working directly on the machine and those in supporting roles. And it collects this information for more than one machine. A single system tracks their efforts for all machines which can highlight dependent issues between multiple production lines and support staff.

Now, just as temperature and pressure data can be analyzed to fine tune the performance and quality of the machine, workforce data such as labor availability, skills, tenure and unplanned absenteeism are analyzed to improve the availability, performance and quality of the labor supporting the operation.

A workforce management system delivering the details that power the OLE metric provides management with the ability to identify subtle issues that add to an operation's losses. Listed below are some common labor related production issues. To identify these issues manually would require collecting the detailed information on all of the individuals associated with the operation during the period of time in question. To do this employee schedules, production schedules, production results, HR personnel information and timecards of all the people associated with the operation during that period of time are required. After it is collected, it all must be reconciled, for example, who was working on the machine when there was more than three hours of downtime over the past month? And what was their tenure?

Availability

Start up issues

- New supervisor

- Attendance issues

- Returning from lunch late

Downtime

- Poorly scheduled lunches and breaks with no coverage

- Team meetings held during critical periods of production

- Maintenance team is unavailable

Performance

- Operators with low hours of experience on this machine

- Labor Standards aren't accurate

Quality

- Too much overtime is wearing operators out, causing errors

- Turnover in this department is higher than average

Manually pulling the details of production together to identify areas of opportunity is not only inefficient in terms of time spent, it can also be ineffective. The person gathering and reconciling the labor data will screen out pieces of the data they feel aren't necessary to the analysis to save time. The logic makes sense. Why collect and organize the data if the information might not be used? This built-in bias to collecting data is how opportunities to make improvements are missed.

Collecting and aggregating data from multiple shifts and departments becomes such a major effort that continuous improvement projects are focused on issues that are supported by easily available data. Workforce management simply expands what's easily available.

82% =	Availability 87%	X	Performance 95%	X	Quality 99%
Machine information tracked through OEE	Scheduled availability • Offline • Cleaning • Product changeover Downtime reason codes • Tooling • Waiting • Adjustment • No operator		Machine attributes • Pressure, temp/voltage • Cycle time • Nameplate performance Machine status • Run • Cycle/jog • Stop		Work order/Part number Yield Quality reason codes Machine operator
Labor information tracked through OLE	Scheduled availability • Breaks • Planned leave Unplanned absence • Attendance policies • Qualified substitutes Maintenance details • Response time • Duration of repair/setup Downtime reason codes • Tooling • Waiting • No operator		Operator info • Skills and certifications • Tenure • Turnover • Training hours • Labor standard history Cost performance • Actual wage • Overtime/premium pay On time delivery performance Cycle time analysis • Historical performance • Standards history		Work order/Part number Yield Quality reason codes Corrective action history Operator info • Skills and certifications • Tenure • Turnover • Training hours Supervisor/operator schedule patterns

The chart above shows the typical information available that can be used to analyze the losses in an operation when OLE is measured in a workforce management system.

Measuring Labor Cost Performance at an Operation

In addition to labor details such as tenure and skills, OLE can also measure the cost performance of an operation. If costs aren't closely measured at an operation, they can creep up as the focus is placed on OEE and OLE scores. Increasing the availability of maintenance or staffing the operation with the most highly skilled operators is tempting to improve the effectiveness of production, but the potential increase in profits can unknowingly leak out through increased payroll costs.

Below are some factors that affect the cost of production for operators and indirect labor used to support the equipment:

- Often a fixed wage standard is applied to cost, but the reality is actual wages can fluctuate significantly due to wage differences, overtime and shift premiums.

- The amount of time maintenance is spending on the machine to keep it running. This cost is invisible to an OEE calculation, but spending an increased amount of money on maintenance to keep a machine running can drive up costs that are not accurately reflected in the profitability of the product.

- The number of staff actually used to operate the line or machine.

It took a little while longer than expected, but Graham and the production manager were able to put together a comprehensive profile of all the people that worked on the press operation. They included the production leads as well. They had also pulled from the workforce management system the tenure, skills and time spent in the department. It was then that they saw a trend. Graham could see why there was no pattern in the production data they had reviewed previously: the variability was contained within the labor data. When both the production lead and the operator had less than six months experience, either the quality or the performance dropped. If either one had significant experience the operation ran smoothly. While all had been trained and certified on the operation, apparently there were still some skills to be learned through experience.

While Graham wasn't sure how to solve this problem, he at least now knew a number of options:

- *Poka-yoke the fixture to eliminate the variation by operator.*

- *Increase the level of experience required to run or supervise the press and add that as a scheduling rule.*

- *Identify the missing skills and improve the training.*

More importantly Graham realized that even with the timekeeping records and the electronic schedules, to really get down into the details of what was causing production losses, they needed to track how labor was applied to production. This manual data collection exercise took a couple of days just to identify one issue at a machine. He would never get to his 10% goal this way.

When Graham shared his thoughts with supervisors and operators about the need for more data collection the production managers were worried about the impact on production. Operators were concerned that the information would be used against them.

But as they walked through some scenarios, they all realized it wasn't as much data collection as they originally thought. For example, in some cases an operation had already been successfully optimized. For those operations, they only needed to capture the occasional downtime issues. Graham also committed to working with the Information Technology department to reconfigure their work order travelers and install barcode readers to reduce keyboard data entry. This would allow operators to simply swipe in and out of an operation in less than two seconds. With some additional suggestions they all agreed to try it in one department to see how it would work.

Making Better Investment Decisions Using the OLE Metric

There are many attributes of the workforce that companies would like to improve. And these often require investments. Take turnover for example. While some amount of turnover is good in order to maintain wage levels and cycle people through who are no longer happy with their roles, too much can degrade performance and quality. It is difficult to know how much is too much. Without the ability to link the HR metric of turnover to the production metrics of performance and quality, it's difficult to provide an answer.

The same applies to training. While most production employees will provide positive feedback to the quality of training, it is difficult to assess whether the financial investment in terms of training costs and lost time in production was worth it. Did the team that was trained actually improve their effectiveness? And if they did, when does turnover require a new training?

Measuring OLE can provide insight to those and other decisions about investing in the workforce. OLE is the link between the difficult to measure Human Capital attributes and production output metrics.

By looking at OLE after an investment in training, or a retention effort to reduce turnover, the picture becomes clear. These investments either paid off with an increase in Overall Labor Effectiveness or they did not.

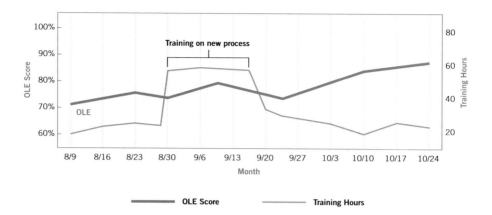

The chart above shows training investment and OLE value over time. If the goal of the training session is to improve effectiveness, then OLE should improve after the training has been completed.

The Elliott Company is a good example of a company that has used its ERP and workforce management systems to generate daily and weekly performance metrics down to the individual operation level.

Elliott Company

Elliott Company is a manufacturer of large rotating equipment for the petro-chemical industry. Manufacturing these products takes a significant amount of highly skilled labor. And a job can take several months to more than a year to complete. Elliott has extended the use of its workforce management system in a variety of ways beyond simple time tracking for payroll. It also tracks labor on the production floor, providing reconciliation of payroll hours to production hours.

This information is used to understand productive hours versus unproductive hours which contain both waste and necessary indirect hours. Indirect hours are not always a waste that can be eliminated. For example, unavoidable labor such as cleaning is not directly attributable to a work order but still an important part of operations. "Indirect spending is easily monitored in our workforce management system so we know exactly where our labor dollars are being used," explains John Russo, Senior Business Systems Analyst with the Elliott Company.

Another use of the information is to understand the status of the job. Because the products can take a year to complete and on-time delivery is critical, Elliott can also measure the current state of production and through labor standards, predict the completion date for a specific uncompleted operation. Measurement of actual versus standard is a key metric in cost analysis which Elliott uses throughout the life of the job. The information is also valuable in quoting future orders. This also allows the company to add or change resources long before it becomes close to the due date. This may result in less overtime near the end of a job and help keeps it on time.

Elliott frequently makes custom products and as a result often must estimate labor standards used for quoting prices and lead times. By analyzing the actual production time of similar parts, estimates on labor standards are fairly accurate and result in better pricing and lead-time projections.

In the machine shop, the supervisor uses the workforce management system to improve the service Elliott provides to customers. When a part breaks but is not kept in inventory by Elliott, it needs to be machined... and quickly. The customer is experiencing expensive downtime and wants to get its production online again. The shop supervisor receives frequent expediting calls from customers looking to find out the status of their replacement part. By querying the workforce management system with the job number of that replacement part, he can see exactly where the job is in its routing and provide an accurate estimate of time to completion to the customer. All this is accomplished within a minute and without leaving his desk. This fast response time and improved accuracy of delivery estimates is a service that differentiates Elliott from its competitors. Because the workforce management system can also track the status of the work in process, Elliott does not have to implement a Manufacturing Execution System in parallel to its workforce management system to provide this querying ability.

Graham was feeling the wear and tear of the last couple of months but they had made significant progress:

- *Individual operations within production had been evaluated and the correct frequency and granularity of data required to identify losses had been determined.*

- *The Information Technology department had reconfigured the information on work order travelers to add barcodes. Data entry terminals were added where needed to the production floor based on feedback from the production teams that included the operators who would be collecting the data.*

- *Operators had been educated on why the data collection was required and how it would be used. Special attention had been paid to ensure operators* benefitted from changing the way they reported production such as the elimination of paper forms.

- Reports had been developed to communicate the desired key performance indicators to different areas of production.

The effort to change processes and behaviors in order to collect more information around operations was challenging. Graham did ask the CEO, Spencer to come in and speak with the unions because there was significant resistance to the changes at first. The unions were concerned that the information would be used to eliminate jobs. Spencer explained that the market was growing and if they could reduce costs, the company could grow and add jobs, but at the current cost structure the company was not competitive and was losing market share. He stressed that his objective was to do more with the same number of people and not to eliminate jobs. This had helped the union understand why the change was required. Over time, they increasingly became cooperative and even began making suggestions for improvements.

Each time a process was changed there was some initial pain, but as the weeks went on, it just became a part of the new routine. In many cases individuals themselves benefited from the changes. Supervisors weren't constantly questioning why a decision was made and the reduction in time spent filling out multiple paper forms was a big relief for the operators. Graham held to his commitments to the union. When the data collection administrators were no longer needed to manage the paper forms and enter the production data into multiple systems, they had been trained at specific operations and added to production, allowing for increased capacity at no additional labor cost.

It had been eight months now, and with the improvement projects identified to be complete by the end of the year, Graham felt comfortable that they could increase production capacity by several percent through reducing labor driven losses that were constraining operations. As he recorded the increases in throughput, he calculated that the capacity increase along with the previous labor cost reductions would reduce unit cost by almost 6%. But he still needed another 4% to reach his 10% goal.

USING LABOR INFORMATION TO MAKE
OPERATIONAL DECISIONS

Operational Expense Reductions	
2.5% reduction in payroll inflation in operations	$5,000,000
Premium pay reduction	$9,000,000
Medical insurance premium reduction	$2,000,000
Improved labor scheduling	$12,000,000
Throughput Increases	
Reduced downtime - production increase	25,000 units

Through the last couple of months, Graham had been interacting closely with other departments and spending more time with a wider variety of people in his own organization. He noticed that for the first time production had better information than other departments. He repeatedly explained to other departments the concepts of Lean Labor as a prelude to why he needed the changes he was requesting. He thought about all the progress his team had made in the last nine months focused on labor and wondered if there were opportunity for those departments to streamline their own processes as well. He knew personnel costs made up a significant portion of the overhead that contributed to unit cost.

CHAPTER 6

INCREASING THE PRODUCTIVITY OF THE ENTIRE WORKFORCE

■■■■

Graham was a little surprised at how much the other departments had grown over the years. Almost a third of the company's employees were not in production roles. From purchasing to maintenance, thousands of employees were needed to support production and the business processes of the company. He knew these departments had a mix of hourly and salaried employees and that many performed fairly repetitive tasks similar to a production environment. For many departments, the hourly wages for these positions were even higher than for production employees.

He was also surprised by the number of contractors the company hired. He knew that many worked in his department to help flex the size of his workforce, but their time tracking had always been managed separately from the full time production employees. He wondered if he could apply the principles of the Perfect Paycheck to contractors as well.

He hadn't counted on reducing costs in the other departments as a part of his esti-mates, but now saw it as a realistic and necessary goal. Graham sent an email to the other department heads inviting them to a short meeting to learn about Lean Labor.

While most companies begin their Lean efforts in production, many have also seen the opportunities off the production floor. Lean can be ap-plied to any business process including industries outside of manufacturing.

The following table shows examples of the breakdown of employee roles in several different industries and highlights the opportunity to improve labor performance outside of production.

	Engine, Turbine, and Power Transmission Manufacturing	Meat Processing	Pharmaceutical Manufacturing	Utilities
EMPLOYEE ROLE				
Production	58%	70%	29%	2%
Installation, Maintenance and Repair	7	5	4	29
Administration	8	4	11	18
Transportation and Material Movement	3	15	3	2
Life, Physical and Social Sciences	<1	<1	20	2
Architectural and Engineering	11	<1	5	11
Business and Financial Operations	3	<1	7	7
Sales	2	1	3	1
Management	6	2	11	7

Source: Bureau of Labor Statistics

Shown above are some examples of workforce percentages by industry by role. It's easy to see a large percentage of labor cost can occur outside of a production line, but labor allocation also varies widely by industry.

While support staff costs are managed at a high level, often as a percentage of budget or headcount for example, it's rare to manage their efficiency to the same degree as a production operator.

Some departments can yield more savings than others. Departments with repetitive tasks and non-exempt employees are the first priority because they are the closest to a repetitive production environment. Accuracy in accruals and time off requests is a good first step with exempt employees such as purchasing, finance and IT.

Following are examples of how Lean Labor can be used to identify and capture those gains. In all cases manufacturers have successfully found ways to standardize work processes and cut waste out of these supporting roles while still maintaining service levels.

Contract Employees

Primarily used for flexing the workforce temporarily or acquiring expensive skills that are needed for a specific task, companies use contract labor for a variety of reasons, from providing design services, to staffing up holiday production lines, to harvesting fields.

The agreements for temporary employees may be with an employment agency or with individual contractors. The relationships vary, but they typically differ from a supplier relationship because the hiring company takes on the risk of contract employee's performance. Because of this, the company needs to increase its visibility into and control over these relationships.

Frequently contract labor is managed manually or on a different system than full time labor. Due to this, some challenges in managing and coordinating the efforts of contract labor can occur:

- Reconciling the actual hours worked by the contract employees and the invoice sent by the employment agency.

- Providing for the safety of the contract employees while on premise. Depending on the size of the facility and the access points, it can be challenging to even know who is on premise. In the event of a safety incident, it's important to be able to quickly account for all people on site. Additionally if the contract employee is not behaving safely, it is important to be able to document this and terminate the agreement.

- Understanding when to expand or shrink the number of contract employees based on production demand and the availability of full time employees.

- Identifying underperforming contract employees or those with attendance problems.

Progressive manufacturers and temporary employment agencies have solved these issues by capturing contract labor hours on the same timekeeping system as the full-time employees. A report of the contract employee's worked hours can be exported and sent to the agency as the agreed record of hours worked. Through automation the timekeeping, billing, and reconciliation of time worked and invoiced is easy. This benefits both the company and the employment agency because less time is spent reconciling and negotiating the billed hours. Payments can also be delivered faster to the agency. This extension of the manufacturer's timekeeping system to track contract employees can be a point of negotiation when determining the premium for providing the contract service.

Aside from invoicing, with all the labor hours in one system, it becomes easy to look at production against all labor hours and determine if more or less contract labor is needed should demand for product or service change.

Safety is improved as well. With all employees clocked into the timekeeping system, creating a muster sheet becomes a click of the button. Just as performance can be measured, so can safety incidents and other on-the-job policies in the workforce management system. Tracking contract employees is especially important when safety is critical because some contract employees who have been terminated due to safety or performance issues will move from agency to agency to get back onto a site. By maintaining employee records for contract employees, it becomes easier for a company to identify these individuals.

With plants that are located in smaller towns where the same seasonal workers return year after year, this data can be used to determine the performance of the contract employee as well. Attendance, safety and productivity can be measured and these results can build a "prioritized" list with the agency or identify the best candidates to bring on full time when there is an opening.

Aker Philadelphia Shipyard is a great example of a company that has used workforce management technology to improve the value it receives from its contract labor. Aker uses contractors to provide specialized welding skills. Both contract employees and full time employees use the same workforce management systems to track their time, attendance and safety incidents. Additionally, labor standards have been developed for each job to measure performance. To streamline the invoicing and payment process for contract agencies, Aker prints out the hours worked by the contractors and uses that record of time as the basis for what should be paid. In doing this, it has reduced the previously manual process of reconciling the contracting company's invoice with the paper time sheets from four days to one hour. In addition, because labor standards are maintained for each job, Aker can quickly identify when an inexperienced contract employee is supplied even though Aker is paying an "experienced" rate. This performance rating as well as safety incident and attendance records are used during contract negotiations to justify the contract labor rate and exclude certain individuals from working at Aker.

Additionally, due to the accuracy of its labor standards, Aker can project its labor needs in advance by skill so the contract agencies have time to provide the right labor, and Aker doesn't keep contractors on payroll when they are not required.

Material Handlers, Quality Control and Other Indirect Staff Supporting Production

Employees such as material handlers and those in quality control often support multiple product lines and are categorized as indirect labor. Their costs are allocated to overhead rather than directly to each unit of a product. As a consequence, indirect labor is often not measured as closely as time associated with production operators. This accounting technique has given rise to a loop hole for production managers under extreme pressure to reduce labor costs. This loop hole allows production managers to re-categorize activities into indirect tasks so their costs are shared among multiple products. If this is not identified by accounting or their managers, the product costs become skewed.

Additionally, with less focus on performance, these indirect employees do not always receive the same attention from continuous improvement efforts as do direct employees. While traditional shop floor systems focus on the value added (or direct) operations, workforce management accurately tracks the activities of both the direct and indirect labor. This visibility to the entire process provides opportunities for improving utilization and efficiency to all the labor supporting the main processes.

Maintenance Mechanics

The objective of maintenance is to make sure equipment is operating properly to ensure high availability and peak performance. Ideally, this should be driven through scheduled maintenance with the occasional need to fix equipment that unexpectedly shuts down. Yet many maintenance mechanics are treated like firemen, responding to urgent calls throughout the day.

Total Productive Maintenance (TPM) provides an effective methodology to ensure maximum uptime and performance of equipment. Workforce management can play a role in helping achieve those goals by delivering accurate raw data. While many machines have Programmable Logic Controllers (PLC's) that capture information about the machine's uptime and downtime, there are just as many machines that do not have PLC's and required manual data collection. As a result companies capturing data manually do this through their workforce management system.

Compounding the complexity of collecting maintenance data is the number of individuals providing maintenance to equipment. Some manufacturers have trained production operators to also provide maintenance on the line for small issues. This practice also tends to have lower labor costs as production operators are typically less skilled and have lower wages than a maintenance mechanic. By tracking both direct and indirect positions in one system, the number of software applications on the production floor is reduced, training is simplified and the data resides in one database.

Analysis is also improved because a complete record of the downtime and corrective action that has occurred is recorded for all employees who have touched the equipment and dependent issues can be identified.

Examples of root cause issues that can be identified from workforce data include:

- Do specific operators or products cause more downtime than others?

- Is the machine worn out and is repairing it now more expensive than replacing it?

- Are mechanics working on non-constraint equipment rather than prioritizing constrained operations first?

- Does maintenance respond quickly, but with repairs that don't last?

- Is the maintenance department understaffed, or do they have low productivity?

Some companies use Computerized Maintenance Management Systems (CMMS) or Enterprise Asset Management (EAM) in conjunction with workforce management. In these cases CMMS or EAM control and issue the materials and work orders for maintenance and the workforce management system collects the results against that issued work.

Warehouse Labor

Labor is the number one variable cost in a warehouse. Warehouse management systems (WMS) do a great job of "moving product." But they are not typically designed to schedule, track, cost, and manage labor through the day. Especially if that labor is being used to perform value-added operations outside of the traditional pick, pack, ship, receive and put-away operations.

The following is an example of a company that successfully used its workforce management system to deliver better labor information. This company distributes components from an inventory of hundreds of thousands of stock keeping units (SKU's). It also offers value-added services such as kitting, and assembly. In this competitive market it differentiates itself by offering same day shipping on parts currently in inventory. For orders received by 3 o'clock in the afternoon, it will ship the same day

99.9% of the time. This means it has at minimum four hours to receive an order and put the component on the truck that pulls away from the dock at 7 PM every day.

Same-day shipping is a valued service to customers and the business is growing. But the company was running out of warehouse space. And to extend the warehouse to handle the extra volume would take well over a year. A second challenge was the company wasn't sure what its cost was for delivering the value added service such as kitting. It made a best estimate and set a price for the service.

These issues drove the VP of Operations to look into ways of finding capacity in the existing building and getting a better handle on labor productivity and costs.

As the company looked at its existing workforce management system and warehouse management system, it realized that each system was collecting granular information about the business. Workforce management knew all about employees' time and schedules, or the labor capacity of the operation. And the warehouse management system was managing the release of the work into the operation, the labor demand. As the operation grew, relying on the supervisors to manage the balance of labor demand and labor capacity manually was becoming less effective. A supervisor could manage his own department, but it was difficult to look across multiple departments to understand where there was excess capacity that could be redeployed elsewhere. Supervisors needed the ability to see where all warehouse employees were located and what the demand was for their labor. If they had this view, they could then shift individuals around throughout the day to increase productivity.

The company decided to reconcile the labor capacity data from its workforce management system with the demand data from the warehouse management system. The company created a "15-minute" report that showed its supervisors which locations in the warehouse were overstaffed and which were understaffed, allowing supervisors to easily identify and move people from any department throughout the day. The beauty of this solution is that it didn't require any additional data collection because the employee ID, location and work order were already being captured in the hand-held barcode scanners. This new report resulted in no re-education or changes in process for the warehouse employees and significant productivity gains for the company.

Warehouse Monitor

		Items In Queue	Std Minutes In Queue	Total Items Required	Std Hours Required	Current Labor Required	Labor / Demand Variance
⊟ Pack	Location						
▷	⊞ MG	0	0.00	200	2.09	3.19	1.10
🔔	⊞ MN	4	3.45	100	1.44	0.00	-1.44
▷	⊞ MO	16	11.63	900	10.91	19.14	8.23
🔔	⊞ MP	0	0.00	300	5.89	0.00	-5.89
▷	⊞ MR	1	0.63	10	0.10	3.19	3.08
▷	⊞ MS	2	1.29	60	0.65	3.19	2.54
⊟ Pick	Location						
🔔	⊞ LG	0	0.00	650	6.50	0.00	-6.50
○	⊞ LN	18	11.78	570	6.22	6.38	0.16
🔔	⊞ LO	0	0.00	210	2.27	0.00	-2.27

The image above is an example of a real-time warehouse monitoring dashboard.

Field Employees

Field based employees are a broad group including sales executives and service employees. While companies often track time worked including time-off request processes in a workforce management system for all field based employees, tracking activities is more common in workforce management systems for service employees. Examples of these types of employees are those who provide installation of products or follow-up warranty or maintenance work. Because their primary value-add is labor which is measured by time, a workforce management system is often a good fit for accurately calculating pay and hours worked while delivering continuous improvement information in terms of time management. These types of employees are typically work order driven, allowing time to be measured against discrete jobs. Additionally it is relatively easy to track employee hours either through a mobile device or at the end of the day where they enter their information through a PC.

The same utilization and performance metrics can be gained from this information as with other types of employees. But the unique value companies receive from moving field employees from a paper-based system of work orders and tickets is the speed and accuracy with which a customer can be invoiced, improving cash flow. One oil and gas equipment manufacturer created an interface back to its ERP system and used the time and work details to also populate its customer invoices. This change eliminated the second manual entry into the ERP system because it was now automatically copied from the workforce management system daily. The change meant reducing the delay between field work performed and invoice issued from three weeks to one week with a significant improvement in cash flow as a result.

Research & Design

Before the first welding torch is lit or molding machine warmed up, many companies expend significant time and expense working with customers to design a product. For those Engineer-to-Order (ETO) products where the design of each product can take a couple of hours to months, the design and tool building processes are really the front end of the production process; therefore measuring the capacity, cost and productivity of this step is an important consideration.

But even after initial design, engineering costs continue to accrue. Ongoing maintenance engineering costs for supporting other functions such as purchasing, production and quality can all be considered variable costs that should be attributed to a product line or customer. But because these can be difficult to track and tie back to a product, they are often added into overhead costs.

New products which often include cutting-edge technology or production techniques generally absorb large amounts of research and engineering time, with the general assumption that these costs will diminish as production becomes stable. If these are considered indirect costs, a longer-than-expected introduction can build in cost that becomes shared across all products and these new products can survive unprofitably for years. While they look fine by standard cost-accounting metrics, the costs associated with constant re-engineering and quality assurance issues are being spread across all products. Champions of the product can point to cost accounting to keep their line alive while others are frustrated that resources are being pulled away from more profitable initiatives. Rather than waiting for executive exhaustion on a product line that is draining resources, understanding the true cost and making informed decisions earlier frees up resources to focus their efforts on the next new product.

In highly commoditized markets, companies can differentiate themselves by using their engineers as a service differentiator. The sales force will often find a sales opportunity that is very close to a standard product, but requires a small customization to meet a customer specification. For companies that have engineering teams organized to deliver long term projects or have limited understanding of their engineering costs, these opportunities can be missed because of long response times or the estimated additional cost assigned is so large the product prices itself out of the market.

For companies involved in basic research, the ability to understand labor costs and where resources are allocated quickly is an important aspect of project management. As target markets change and re-evaluation of investments and resource allocation is required, accurate labor data is important to decision making.

In the life sciences industry, identifying underutilized resources or labor constraints such as lab technicians can shorten development times resulting in longer periods of patent protection for medical devices and pharmaceuticals.

Finally, for companies that perform research such as defense contractors and pharmaceutical companies, many tax authorities around the world such as the Internal Revenue Service (IRS) in the U.S. currently provide tax credits under certain conditions. These claims are often audited, and the IRS looks for information that was gathered contemporaneously with the research taking place. In terms of level of detail, a workforce management system has the ability to accurately track time to specific projects and the time audit details are often used by manufacturers to justify credits and losses.

Using labor data to improve decision making across the extended supply chain

When a supplier sends the wrong part or poor-quality materials, rework or extra handling for the receiving company results. Because this is "out of process" labor, it is a labor variance that is difficult to track and measure.

As suppliers work closely with their customers to shrink the supply chain, there are often agreements made in terms of service or quality that can reduce costs for both parties. One example is a purchase agreement that was made between a portable generator manufacturer and its supplier. As a part of this purchasing agreement, the suppliers guarantee 100% quality in return for higher component prices. As a result, the manufacturer can eliminate incoming inspection. Even with this agreement in place, issues arise from time to time. When issues occur, the company tracks the labor expended in rework and handling within its workforce management system, and back-charges the supplier. Because there is a detailed audit trail, this eliminates negotiation. The company applies the same techniques to capital equipment still under a warranty contract. The time the maintenance department spends repairing the equipment is tracked in its workforce management system and charged back to the company providing the equipment.

The company also tracks labor to understand which components it should purchase and which it should build. The costs between make and buy are often close, but because of the thin margins on the final product, even a couple of pennies makes a difference and the same component can change between purchased and built in-house from year to year depending on supplier quotes. Because the company is confident in its labor costs, it knows it's making good build versus buy decisions.

Graham found that extending the Lean labor principles to other departments was easier now because they had examples of success already. Attention from their CEO didn't hurt either. Because payroll already had many of the processes and reports in place for operations, it was easy to extend them to the other departments. While premium pay and other union rules didn't cause as much variability in employee paychecks as in operations, they were able to quickly reduce 3% of payroll for the 30% of the employees in the company who don't work in production. A significant portion of this was through cleaning up accruals. Based on the last several months, this savings was projected at $2.6 million annually. More importantly, there were a few Lean Labor converts in the other departments that had started looking at their processes more closely and had come back to Graham for advice. He knew that more savings would follow as the rest of the company followed operation's lead in reducing waste not only in labor costs but by improving their throughput.

These changes had created a new challenge for Graham. Other departments were now coming to production, well armed with accurate information about how production was increasing costs for their departments. It was tempting to ignore it, but he knew that with their new found data and Lean thought processes, they were right and he would have to think about how to work more closely with them.

The reduction in contractor costs along with increased R&D tax credits resulted in $2.5 million in savings. With these overhead reductions in place, they had reduced unit costs by 6.3%. Graham updated his records:

Operational Expense Reductions	
2.5% reduction in payroll inflation in operations	$5,000,000
Premium pay reduction	$9,000,000
Medical insurance premium reduction	$2,000,000
Improved labor scheduling	$12,000,000
Payroll inflation reduction in overhead	$2,600,000
Contractor costs & tax credits	$2,500,000
Throughput Increases	
Reduced downtime - production increase	25,000 units

The company had released its quarterly earnings report and investors were pleased. Spencer, their CEO, was confident enough in the progress made so far that he was providing anecdotes of their Lean efforts during financial analyst calls.

Graham had spent a significant portion of his days coaching other departments on how to use Lean to improve their processes, but now that they were headed in the right direction he wanted to get back to the plant and see how things were progressing.

CHAPTER 7

IMPROVING DAILY OPERATIONAL DECISION MAKING

The weekly production meeting was under way when Graham joined. The department supervisors were taking turns sharing the status of the work in their departments. What surprised Graham was that instead of the production control manager writing the status of the work orders on a white board, they were scrolling down a computer screen that displayed each work order along with details such as the current operation, whether it was active or not and its estimated time to completion. Labor metrics were also displayed such as efficiency and cost compared to budget.

The meeting wrapped up several minutes early and after the supervisors left, Graham asked the production control manager how he'd captured the production status electronically.

"We realized that as a by-product of tracking what the production operators are doing at an operational level, we also know the status of the WIP and the machines. We worked with IT and rather than viewing labor centric reports, we turned the data around and now we can also see the status of the machines or the materials at any time. It's eliminated the need for the supervisors to walk around and collect the status of all the released work before every meeting or any time they are asked a question about the status of something on the floor. It also helps my team because we don't have to walk the floor every time customer service calls to see if we can expedite an order. We just pull up the status on the screen and see what's possible."

Process Visibility

Some Lean proponents claim that Lean is best executed by walking the floor and spending time where the work occurs. This is true to a point, but what happens when dependent operations aren't within walking distance? Or if a manager is visiting another plant and wants to see how an important work order is progressing?

Lean is about seeing the entire process to understand the dependencies of changes made in one operation on the next operation. As production speeds up, is it reasonable to expect operators and department supervisors to use clipboards and spreadsheets to manage their operations when every other aspect of their job from production scheduling through metal cutting has been accelerated due to the adoption of new technology?

Supervisors who aren't aware that a piece of equipment was down for four hours or that there were too many people on the line the day before can't be expected to resolve those issues. Additionally, without a record of what happened in one area it's difficult to understand the impact on a dependent operation that takes place two days later.

Improving process visibility is unique for each company. Some can merge the data they are already collecting while others may need to increase the information they collect and then distribute to a wider audience.

By tracking the actual labor and work individuals and teams are performing against the production schedule, real time visibility is available. This provides an accurate view of labor, WIP and machine status at any point in time. The following are a few examples of questions that can be answered on any released work in real time.

- Which operation is currently active?

- Who is currently working on a specific operation?

- What is the yield?

- What is the labor efficiency in this operation?

- What is the cause of the machine downtime, and how long has it been down?

- What was the actual cost of labor spent on this work order?

- Based on the labor standards, what is the estimated completion time of this operation?

- What work is late relative to due date?

- Which jobs should have been started, but are not, and are now jeopardizing on-time delivery?

With visibility into production through the workforce management system, supervisors no longer have to manually track down the status of work prior to a production meeting. This means more time for management by supervisors and production status is always current and available.

Browse Activities by Due Date						
Activity		Status	State	Planned Compl Date	Hrs To Compl	Percent Compl
This Week:						
1222	ACME Drilling					
1999	ACME Drilling					
FORMING: Fill Molds		Open	✓	04/27/2006	49.90	58.42%
SECONDARY OPS: Debur Castings		Open	✓	05/03/2006	46.13	59.89%
SECONDARY OPS: Sandblast		Open	●	05/08/2006	115.00	0%
SECONDARY OPS: Mill Input-Output Ports		Open	●	05/15/2006	120.00	0%
Quality Assurance: Final Inspection		Open	△	05/20/2006	120.00	0%
Next Week:						
1111	TLC Pumping					
Due in 2 Weeks:						

Example of Work in Process status in a workforce management system.

With the ability to see the entire process, supervisors can see the work headed their way from upstream operations and make adjustments when they see delays or more work than they expected.

Adjusting to fluctuating work is nothing new for supervisors. Their challenge is that they are limited to reacting to these changing demands because they have just a few labor options; they may use overtime or make adjustments to the labor currently within their department. These options are narrowed further by work rules such as seniority or bumping. With electronic labor tracking, the supervisor has visibility to everyone on the shop floor and may be able to find someone qualified and available at regular wage while still meeting all the work rules. Or if they have excess labor, rather than sending someone home, they may be able to transfer the person to a department that needs them.

Applying Controls and Alerts to the Process

In addition to tracking status and calculating metrics such as efficiency and yield, workforce management systems have also built in controls to assist in improving the quality of the process. As an example of jidoka, or "automation with a manual touch," workforce management can track the sequencing and production results of an operation and at defined limits, stop operators from continuing without supervisor intervention. This can be implemented in several ways.

- Checks can be applied to each operation in the routing to ensure that none are performed out of sequence. This is a big benefit when there are new people in production unfamiliar with the operation or new products are introduced regularly.

- The status of released work can be changed remotely. An example of this is when an urgent engineering change needs to be processed and production should stop until the change can be incorporated.

- A scrap limit on the process can be defined. For example, "stop the process if more than five percent bad parts are reported."

By automating these controls new operators require less supervision and when quality limits change, there isn't a learning curve as operators become familiar with the new levels, they are automatically enforced.

Additionally, because workforce management systems can track labor activities, they can also track the corrective actions that took place to improve quality. Old processes can be compared to new processes to determine if labor efficiencies and costs really improved or not. The ability to capture and compare changes is important to continuous improvement efforts along with capturing the evolution of knowledge that can be lost during turnover and retirement.

Ceradyne Incorporated is an example of a manufacturer that has built a workforce management system that has resulted in operational improvements from a better understanding of the 4M's.

Ceradyne Incorporated

Ceradyne, a manufacturer of highly technical ceramic products, has products for a wide variety of industries from fuel pump rollers to dental brackets for orthodontic braces, to body and vehicle armor for the military.

As a part of a contractor's agreement with the Department of Defense, a manufacturer will record the direct labor involved for each contract with the government. Ceradyne originally tracked these details on paper, which was time consuming for Ceradyne's employees. It took several administrators to collate, track down and correct missing or illegible time tickets. Mark Nguyen, the IT Project Manager at Ceradyne recognized that by sending the production schedule from the ERP system to the workforce management system Ceradyne could accurately collect production time against each operation and contract, collecting two of the four M's, Man and Method. By collecting production results from each operation defined by the routing, the third M, Materials is captured and then shared with Ceradyne's ERP system for back-flushing.

Ceradyne's workforce management system is designed to provide up to date information any time it is requested. To provide this information, the workforce management system interfaces to its ERP system and maintains a copy of the production schedule. By tracking who is working (or not working) on each operation, the current production status of all the plants is available at any point in time from any location. This results in better information for making daily decisions. With the information available to every employee, individuals are empowered to make decisions based on the current situation. This empowerment increases personal responsibility and speeds up the decision making process. As an example, the new information allows supervisors to identify substitute operators from employees currently at the plant without having to resort to temporary workers or call-ins.

Management can see the exact status of each order and who is working on it along with the current performance metrics of utilization, efficiency and quality. This allows them to quickly adjust or notify other departments about changes in production.

Ceradyne has also extended the tracking of resources from employees and Work in Process (WIP) to include machines as well, completing the four M's. The ability to track the performance of the machines allows Ceradyne to better gauge the need for maintenance or additional training for operators.

And because this information is automatically reconciled with the payroll data, time paid but not value-added, such as operators idled while waiting can be identified and reduced.

As a result Ceradyne has improved employee utilization by 5-10%. Jerry Pellizzon, Chief Financial Officer for Ceradyne, explains, "We utilize workforce management to improve the efficiency on a real-time basis for managing our production groups in many different locations. The key result is that we continue to experience improvement in productivity and the reduction of our costs."

It would take some time for all the reports and alerts to be developed and then for the supervisors and operators to get comfortable using them, but Graham could see the potential. The ability to open up the production floor for all to see would eliminate much of the waiting that was occurring.

One other result of better utilization was shorter lead times. While this was already incorporated into the savings it had an even more important market effect. The company was gaining a reputation in the industry for being able to respond to orders more quickly than the competition. And it was now delivering product significantly faster than their offshore competition. Lead times were important to their customers because it allowed them to bring production online faster, improving their return on assets. This tangible benefit helped offset the competition's lower product price because competitors couldn't meet the shorter lead times without premium freight.

Graham saw the first signs of progress in the monthly variance meetings. Throughput was up 1% already and his production managers were ready to commit to another 2% due to the improvements in labor utilization. Better utilization of Work in Process had reduced inventory costs by 1%. Labor costs continued to go down as on-premise employees were better utilized and call-in premiums and overtime were further reduced. A year ago he would have thought this impossible, but as Graham added the 3% increase in throughput and reductions in inventory expense, he was excited to see that unit costs had been reduced by almost 8.5%.

Operational Expense Reductions	
2.5% reduction in payroll inflation in operations	$5,000,000
Premium pay reduction	$9,000,000
Medical insurance premium reduction	$2,000,000
Improved labor scheduling	$12,000,000
Payroll inflation reduction in overhead	$3,500,000
Contractor costs & tax credits	$2,000,000
Reduced labor cost due to improved utilization	$2,600,000
Reduced material costs due to better visibility	$2,500,000
Throughput Increases	
Reduced downtime – production increase	25,000 units
Operational visibility – production increase	15,000 units

Not only were labor variances going down overall, but the variances that were occurring were better understood. During the meeting there was also some discus-

sion about prioritizing work orders. Graham wasn't sure he followed the conversation, rather than interrupt, he walked out with the plant accountant and asked him why the focus on changing the prioritization of the work orders, especially when they had spent so much time and money on automating the production schedule through a software application.

"Walk with me back to the office and I'll explain why." Jack responded.

CHAPTER 8

LABOR COSTING AS A COMPETITIVE ADVANTAGE

"Now that production hours and labor hours are automatically reconciled through the workforce management system, our unexplained labor variances have virtually disappeared. I've been able to balance the books faster than ever before and the monthly variance meetings with the production managers have become civilized," Jack continued.

"Anything to make your job easier, but what was the discussion around prioritizing the jobs on the floor, I thought the production schedule did that for us?" asked Graham.

"That's the problem; it's close but not exact. For as long as I've been here we never had the details of where the labor was being used in production. In accounting we rely on the labor standards to estimate the labor cost in each product, the production schedule uses them to calculate how long a job should take to complete. We know our labor standards can't be completely accurate because of all the variances. So part of our job in accounting is to decide where to allocate those variances and adjust the labor standards as best as we can. The argument with production was always over the value of the labor standards not reflecting the reality on the production floor."

"But if the standards aren't accurate, how good could the production schedule be?" asked Graham.

"Exactly, that's one of the reasons production control and the department supervisors are always massaging the production schedule." Jack answered. Between customers asking for changes, the typical disruptions in production and a production schedule that was tough to meet, it keeps everyone busy rescheduling jobs and moving people throughout the day.

"So how does the workforce management system make that any better?" Graham wanted to know.

"By providing me with a much more accurate picture of where the labor is truly used during production, I don't have to use the peanut butter method of accounting."

"Peanut butter method, what is that?"

"That's an old saying describing a situation where time or costs, in this case labor hours, that can't be directly allocated to a product are spread evenly across all products within a department. This has the effect of artificially increasing the costs of some products and decreasing the costs of others. It also makes updating labor standards difficult because we never really know if the standard is accurate or if production isn't meeting expectation. The only way to resolve it is to bring an industrial engineer in to measure the operation and we can't afford to do that for each task. Now that we have better labor allocation, our standards are improving. This has improved the adherence to our production schedules and also means our labor costs are more accurate. But to answer your original question about prioritization, our supervisors have the flexibility to re-order the production schedules during the day. For example if they have 5 jobs for the day, something may go wrong that forces them to re-order which ones they do next. Some of the supervisors would take advantage of that flexibility and run the easiest jobs first because they know their metrics will look better. Because our product costs weren't that accurate, their decisions were driven by which jobs would increase their labor efficiency the most. But now that we know which products provide the most profit, we can help them to prioritize the products which deliver the most profits to the company. Each decision may not have a big impact, but over the year, delivering higher profit items first improves our cash flow which in turn increases our profitability."

Graham leapt ahead, he was already thinking about the constant discussions he has with the VP of Sales over discounting. He too knew the costs in the ERP system weren't completely accurate. As a result management had devised an approval process when customers asked for large discounts. These steep discounts were often requested when the quantities were large or a hungry competitor was vying for the business. To determine the lowest price that would still be profitable, they would take the direct costs and add 20% to accommodate any additional direct costs that might have been allocated in overhead costs. That calculation was considered a reasonable estimate and generally won the business. The down side was that negative material and labor variances would soar and as a result cash flow would dip when these unprofitable orders came too frequently. With accurate product costs he could make better decisions about what levels of discounts he would approve and more importantly he could explain his decisions in terms of profitability so he didn't get over-ruled by a sales team trying to meet its revenue goal.

He wondered what the impact would be if sales and marketing also had a better understanding of the company's product costs? If sales knew which products provided the most profits, their compensation programs could be adjusted to reward sales of those products. Marketing would know which product lines justified more promotional dollars. Those product lines that weren't contributing enough to profits could finally be identified and margins could be improved through price increases and cost reductions.

Whether a company is pricing out a multi-year project to engineer and construct an oil drilling platform or deciding what products to make today with their raw milk, knowing the true cost of production allows companies to walk away from deals and product lines that can tie up their resources while generating no profit. Two companies could have exactly the same products, machines, materials and even workforce, but the one that makes better product mix and pricing decisions will generate higher profits with those assets.

When calculating product cost, determining the actual contribution of labor cost is the most challenging because labor generates cost in fours ways:

- Base wage

- Premiums, bonuses and other variable components of pay

- Benefit costs

- Labor efficiency (the actual time to produce a product or deliver a service compared to expected)

Adding to the complexity is these are different for each individual and can vary over the duration of production.

A company's ability to track and allocate these costs into product is what separates a company that uses labor costing as a strategic tool versus one that uses a peanut butter accounting method to estimate their product costs. What makes labor costing so difficult is there is no single answer. There is a trade-off between cost of collection and managing a complex cost model versus the benefit to the company.

For a company to develop its own efficient costing model, it needs to understand the decisions its employees will be making with that data. Purchasing, operations, sales, marketing and finance all use product costs to make decisions. A cost that is inaccurate leaks profits every day as sub-par decisions to outsource production, discount products or prioritize production improvements are made. As one of the most variable and controllable components to product cost, generating accurate labor costs is an important component of any costing model.

There are two factors that should be considered when determining how much accuracy is required in labor costing; the impact on profitability and the cost of accuracy.

The Impact of Pricing Decisions on Profitability

Every day employees are forced to fill in gaps of information using experience and intuition or relying on previously made decisions for guidance. If the decision being considered involves a large financial transaction such as purchasing a piece of capital equipment, the project team will invest time to fill in those gaps with facts. Research is conducted around the cost and performance of operators and maintenance. Forecasts are made about volumes required, lot size and machine effectiveness before a decision to invest is made. There are plenty of controls within the decision making process too. Often several layers of management review and approval are required to ensure no mistakes are made.

A more difficult decision that relies on accurate product cost might be whether a non-conforming product should be scrapped or re-worked. What if the labor required to re-work the product is more than the cost of the labor and material to replace it? Would the decision change if the machine that produced the part were currently running at capacity? How is this decision made and how many factors are considered? Due to a lack of accurate information, is the same decision always made?

Another challenging decision that relies on labor cost might be whether to accept a last minute request from a customer. Say this was one of the manufacturer's largest customers and they asked to have a promotional coupon attached to each carton of product. They offer to pay 30 cents per carton but need it completed for tomorrow's shipment. Would that be a profitable add-on to the order? If the production labor were earning overtime to attach the labels would it still be profitable? The investment in better labor cost data for the first scenario of a capital request can be easily justified. A large purchase should have a significant impact on profitability and it's obvious that good information and decision-making controls need to be in place for the best outcome.

Investing in better data for the second and third scenarios might be tougher to justify. If the decision has an impact of less than $1000 how much information should be collected to support that decision? Is it common knowledge that any time the decision is escalated, management always agrees to accept the order?

Successfully empowering employees doesn't simply mean delegating authority to make decisions. Empowerment must also include providing the right tools and information to make good decisions, often without the experience that management might possess. Determining what decisions are important enough to be supported by accurate data is a challenge for all companies. No one would argue that a significant investment to collect accurate data prior to a capital expenditure is justified. The consequences of a poor decision are painful for everyone involved. But poor decision making on the everyday occurrences such as a scrap or rework decision have less and possibly no consequence and therefore don't receive the same attention relative to accurate costing information. How many of these decisions have to occur before profitability is noticeably impacted?

Decision making is like any other process, it has inputs and outputs and just like a production process, a poor decision will result in a defective outcome. Most companies have a progression of controls and supporting information when making financial decisions. For example, as the size of a purchase order increases, the number of approval signatures also increase. This traditional method of protecting the business from poor decisions misses several factors. It doesn't account for the number of times a decision is made. It also assumes that the consequence of the decision is correlated with the size of the transaction.

Those missing factors, frequency and consequence, are either not a part of the decision making process or left for managers and employees to determine on their own as they make daily decisions. This is an opportunity for poor decisions to be made over and over again without anyone understanding the impact to the business.

This situation has been addressed in production environments using a Six Sigma tool called Failure Mode and Effects Analysis or FMEA. This is a tool that originated in 1949 with the publication of a military procedure Mil-P-1629 titled "*Procedures for Performing a Failure Mode, Effects and Criticality Analysis.*" It has since been adopted by the FDA as a part of Good Manufacturing Practice (GMP), the automotive industry in QS9000 and the American Society for Quality Control. FMEA extends analysis from the severity of a defect in a product to include the frequency and the ability to detect that a defect has occurred. It ranks each factor (severity, frequency and ability to detect) with a number from one (small impact, low frequency and easy to detect) to ten (catastrophic failure, high frequency, hard to detect). The mathematical product of these factors is called the Risk Priority Number (RPN). The higher the RPN becomes, the bigger the risk to the company. The benefit to this analysis is that it can uncover a large risk to the company in what seems like a small or unlikely problem.

To use the FMEA tool to analyze decision making risk, substitute the "Process Function" column with "Decision Description." The result of the analysis will be a prioritization of the true impact of a poor decision. With these results, an improved understanding of where profits are leaking due to poor decisions is available. With the information used to generate this analysis, other tools such as poka-yoke and improved information can be used to improve decision making processes and capabilities.

Below is an example of a Failure Modes and Effects Analysis chart that has been completed to compare the potential impact of defects caused by poor business decisions within a company. Completing these charts helps rank the size of the impact because the analysis looks not only at the size of the financial impact but also how easy it is to detect a poor decision.

Decision Description	Potential Failure Mode	Effects of Failure	Severity	Potential Cause of Failure	Occurrence	Controls in Place	Detection	RPN
Capital request – expenditures greater than $100,000	Equipment does not perform to expectation	Lost capacity and increased burden rate	7	Manufacturing process more difficult than originally perceived	2	Design Engineering and Process Engineering teams must both sign off on design documents	3	42
Scrap or re-work decisions	Wrong decision based on conditions	Excess material and labor costs or late orders	4	Labor cost difficult to assess, available capacity on equipment not checked	4	Supervisors must approve decisions involving quantities greater than 50 pieces	5	80
Customer requested services	Labor expense greater than revenues	Reduction in profits	3	Actual labor expense difficult to predict	5	Production control must approve order based on labor estimates	7	105

Failure Mode and Effect Analysis chart applied to decision making.

After filling out the chart it becomes clear that the capital request process is in good shape with an RPN number of 42. The score reflects that while the severity of a poor decision is high, the controls are already in place to stop that from happening.

What this analysis brings into focus is the lack of controls around accepting unprofitable service requests. With the highest RPN score of 105, this analysis highlights a problem in the decision making process to determine if the company should accept a customer requested service. Each opportunity for value-add services may only have a small impact on profits, but the lack of control means that unprofitable requests can be accepted frequently and no one will know where the drag on profits is originating. Employees intuitively feel that servicing a large customer is good for the company, but the facts say that the customer is using its size to intimidate the manufacturer into providing unprofitable services.

As a result of this analysis, a business case can be developed to improve the decision making process. The outcome in this case would be to ensure only profitable add-on orders are accepted.

Reducing Data Collection Costs

One of the most frequent objections to improving decision making capabilities is the cost of collecting improved information. This is also true when it comes to improving the accuracy of labor costs to support decision making. The challenge for many companies is that the four components of labor cost are collected in different areas within the company and are not easily reconciled. Productive labor hours may be captured in the ERP system, unproductive hours are captured in variance spreadsheets, labor wages are generated in timekeeping and payroll, and benefit costs are generated in the human resources application. To reconcile this labor cost data to determine the actual cost to rework a product or keep an extra shift on to deliver value-add services is not worth the impact on the decision.

Interestingly, most companies collect all these costs at some point within their business systems. This data is important to different people within the company, but it has not been collected and organized to support production decisions. The advantage for companies that use workforce management to accurately track labor hours as they are applied to production is that these hours are now in a format that makes it simple to include the four components of labor costs (wages, premium pay, benefits and actual efficiency) when calculating labor hours and costs for work performed. Additionally by using the employee scheduling application, the costs for keeping specific people for another shift can be calculated immediately and accurately before a decision has been made to accept an order for a specific price.

The meetings with sales went better than expected. Armed with improved product cost information, sales recognized that focusing on the products with higher gross margins would help the company achieve its profit targets with lower revenues. The sales management team also challenged Graham to find cost reductions on several of the lower margin lines, noting that competitors must have found ways to reduce costs because they continued to be successful even at those seemingly heavily discounted prices.

Previously, Graham was often on the defensive during these conversations, but this time he didn't mind the give and take on product costs because he knew there were some product lines that could use attention. The difference compared to the past is that this conversation had become specific. Rather than hearing the usual mantra of "our products are more expensive than the competition" from sales, the team was able to identify a manageable number of products that needed attention.

With sales promoting the most profitable items, the product mix began to shift. While the products themselves didn't cost any less to produce, profits grew with the same level of production effort. It was as though he had increased his production by a couple percent, but even better because it required no incremental material or labor costs, this change in product mix resulted in more profits due to increased contribution margin. Spencer agreed that the ability to increase profits through a better product mix was just as effective as reducing costs.

Sitting down at his desk, Graham looked at his calendar for the next week and realized that the board was meeting again and it had been a year since he had been tasked with reducing unit costs by 10%. The board had been updated with progress each quarter, but Spencer wanted to provide them with a summary of the total gains for the year. He had met his goals through an 8.5% reduction in unit cost and an increase in contribution margin of $15 million annually through better product mix decisions. This combination had achieved the end result desired by the board: the stock price was increasing, reflecting the improvement in earnings. Graham began writing the numbers down in preparation for the meeting. As he noted each area of benefit, he realized they had achieved their success by acting on many small ideas rather than waiting for "the big idea" to develop.

Operational Expense Reductions	
2.5% reduction in payroll inflation in operations	$5,000,000
Premium pay reduction	$9,000,000
Medical insurance premium reduction	$2,000,000
Improved labor scheduling	$12,000,000
Payroll inflation reduction in overhead	$3,500,000
Contractor costs & tax credits	$2,000,000
Reduced labor cost due to improved utilization	$2,600,000
Reduced material costs due to better visibility	$2,500,000
Throughput Increases	
Reduced downtime – production increase	25,000 units
Operational visibility – production increase	15,000 units
Increased Contribution Margin	
Improved product mix decisions	$15,000,000

Graham met with Spencer and reviewed the accomplishments all had made to achieve the goal. Spencer was very pleased with the results and profits were growing at record rates. The reduction in lead times meant the company was even more competitive with offshore competition and sales were growing as a result. He was pleased to see the career section of the website was filling with open positions.

Spencer knew there was a wealth of detail behind those numbers and the board would likely ask many questions, so he asked Graham to attend the board meeting and lead the presentation.

The board meeting turned out to be easier than Graham thought. Because the results of his efforts had already begun to positively impact profits after only a few months, Graham had earned credibility with the board. While there had been many questions, Graham found it easy to answer because the members of the board were asking how he had accomplished the savings rather than pressuring him for additional results. During a break Graham was even asked by one of the board members to visit her company to share his ideas.

After he had left the meeting, Graham decided to take a walk through the plant. What had seemed impossible just a year ago now allowed him to believe there was even more potential for the company to improve productivity. As he listened to the familiar sounds of production, Graham's greatest satisfaction came from knowing that he had kept his plants open by tapping into the employees' ability to innovate rather than chasing low wages.

REFERENCES

Introduction

Toyota Motor Manufacturing Kentucky, "The Toyota Production System", http://www.toyotageorgetown.com/tps.asp. Accessed July 12, 2010.

Jonathan Katz, "Ranking Continuous Improvement Methods", *Industry Week*, May 1, 2007.

Productions MAJ, *How It's Made*, Television, Discovery Channel, 2010.

Lean Institute, *"History of Lean"*, http://www.lean.org/WhatsLean/History.cfm. Accessed June 3, 2010.

James Womack, *"The Power of Purpose Process and People"*, webinar, May 1, 2008, http://www.lean.org/events/ppp_may_2008_webinar.html.

Chapter 1

Vikas Bajaj, "Bangladesh, With Low Pay, Moves in on China", *New York Times*, July 16, 2010, Business Section.

David Welch, "Labor unrest in China could be Mexico's Gain", *Bloomberg Business Week*, http://www.businessweek.com/autos/autobeat/archives/2010/06/labor_unrest_in_china_could_be_mexicos_gain.html. Accessed August 20 2010.

Toyota Motor Manufacturing Kentucky. "Toyota Production System Terms", http://www.toyotageorgetown.com/terms.asp. Accessed November 12, 2009.

Rana Foroohar, "How to Build Again", *Newsweek*, http://www.newsweek.com/2010/07/10/how-to-build-again.html. Accessed October 2010.

Chapter 2

Nucleus Research, "*ROI Evaluation Report*", July 2006.

US Department of Labor, "Fair Labor Standards Act", http://www.dol.gov/WHD/flsa/index.htm. Accessed February 21, 2010.

US Department of Labor, "Family Medical Leave Act", http://www.dol.gov/WHD/fmla/index.htm. Accessed February 21, 2010.

W. Melvin Haas III, J.D, Managing Member; Constangy, Brooks & Smith, LLC, "12 Ways to Curb FMLA Abuse", http://hr.blr.com/whitepapers/Benefits-Leave/FMLA-Leave-of-Absence/12-Ways-to-Curb-FMLA-Abuse. Accessed May 15, 2010.

Occupational Safety and Health Administration, "*Standards - 29 CFR*".

Industry Week, "Employee Absenteeism Study", June 2010.

Mercer Health and Benefits LLC, "*Survey on the Total Impact of Employee Absences*", June 2010.

Chapter 3

Steven Greenhouse, "More Workers Face Pay Cuts, Not Furloughs", *New York Times*, August 3, 2010, Business Section.

Chapter 4

Core Practice, "Flexible Shift Scheduling", *IMPO Magazine*, September 2009.

Chapter 5

Robert C. Hanson, *Overall Equipment Effectiveness*, Industrial Press Inc., 2001.

James P. Womack and Daniel T. Jones, *Lean Thinking*, 2nd edition, Free Press; June 10, 2003.

REFERENCES

Chapter 6

An Introduction to Total Productive Maintenance (TPM), J. Venkatesh, *Plant Maintenance*, April 16, 2007.

Internal Revenue Service , *Research Credit Claims Audit Techniques Guide (RCCATG)*, May 2008.

Chapter 7

Eliyahu M. Goldratt, Jeff Cox, *The Goal*, North River Press; 3rd edition, 2004.

Chapter 8

Debra Smith, *The Measurement Nightmare*, The St. Lucie Press, 2000.

Richard A. Brealey, Stewart C. Myers, *Principles of Corporate Finance*, 4th Edition, McGraw Hill, 1991.

Michael L. George, *Lean Six Sigma*, McGraw Hill, 2002.

Percent on time – The percentage of orders that are shipped by the due date.

5 S – The Japanese terms for clean-up in the work environment.

> 1S) 'Seiri' or Sort: separate necessary and unnecessary to eliminate the unnecessary.
>
> 2S) 'Seiton' or Store: everything in its place to be easily located.
>
> 3S) 'Seiso' or Shine: maintaining cleanliness.
>
> 4S) 'Seketsu' or Standardize: procedures and responsibilities.
>
> 5S) 'Shitsuke' or Sustain: making a habit of them.

80/20 rule – Pareto principle stating that 80% of problems come from 20% of causes.

Absorption model (standard costing) – Allocating fixed costs (e.g. plant costs and management) based on labor hours or machine time and variable costs (materials and direct labor in making the product) when determining product costs.

Andon – The Japanese term for signal; in manufacturing, the signal such as lights or a bell notifies workers of either a problem with the production process or quality of a good or the end of a shift.

Audit – Conducting a review or examination of how pay rules or policies were applied in specific time periods.

Audit trail – Step by step documented history of activities and revisions occurring during a business process.

Backflushing – An ERP process of reporting the production quantity of a part number to ascertain the raw materials taken from inventory and labor hours used to complete production.

Batch size – Amount of components processed at one station without a new setup.

Biometrics – A method of finger-scanning employees to confirm the individual clocking in is who they claim to be.

Bottleneck – A resource whose capacity is less than the demand required; the output of the entire production line is set by the output of the bottleneck because it is the slowest operation in the line.

Buddy punch – When an employee has another employee clock in for them, increasing their hours paid, but not actually worked.

Bumping – The process of ascension in jobs during a shift when a person needs to be replaced temporarily. The intent is to ensure the scheduled employees working lower paying jobs have the opportunity to earn more, before the position is offered to someone who was not originally scheduled. The person called in or transferred from another department will then fill the lowest paying job for that shift.

Change management – An organized approach for dealing with organizational change.

Collective bargaining agreement – Legally enforceable document establishing employment conditions between a company's management and employees represented by a union for a given period in time.

Commoditized market – Goods or services have no distinct differentiation (considered equal); usually because they are produced in large quantities by many different businesses.

Compliance risk – Risks to a business (usually financial) that occur from non-conformance with laws, regulations or rules.

Constraint – Some factor that constrains another entity from fulfilling its goal. Commonly applied to an operation in the process that is slowing the output of that process.

Contribution margin – Percentage of profit per unit sold. Calculated by (Revenue-variable costs)/Revenue.

Cost performance – Actual cost divided by estimated costs (as defined by a Cost standard).

Cost to serve – The total cost to provide a good or service to a customer. This includes, but is not limited to, efforts such as design, production, distribution, service, support. The objective of this calculation is to understand the total cost in delivering and supporting a product or service rather than only the production and delivery cost for example.

Cycle time – Period of time to complete on cycle of an operation.

Defect – In manufacturing, an outcome other than the desired result.

Defect rate – The frequency at which products without the desired results are produced.

Design for manufacturability – Team-based approach for designing a product as efficiently as possible; it combines employees from different functional areas in a company such as Design, Production, Distribution and Quality to help reduce the issues surrounding bringing the product to market.

Double scheduling – An employee scheduled to work multiple jobs during the same time period.

Duration reporting – Employee enters the total time spent on a project or task, often at the end of the day or week. There are no specific start and stop times for each entry.

Engineer to order – Custom designed products built to unique customer requirements.

Enterprise Resource Planning (ERP) – Information system used to manage business operations and resources.

Fair Labor Standards Act (FLSA) – U.S. federal legislation that protects employees from unfair labor practices and unsafe working conditions, such as establishing minimum wage, overtime pay, and child labor standards; also known as 'Wages and Hours Bill'.

Family Medical Leave Act (FMLA) – U.S. federal regulation establishing time off for employees based on specific personal circumstances such as caring for a sick family member or newborn, or for adoption or foster care of a child.

Gaming the clock – When employees figure out the rounding rules and adjust their behavior by clocking in and out to maximize pay and minimize work. This results in overtime or results in disruption of production.

Gaussian curve – Curve showing normal distribution; also known as "bell curve".

General ledger – A business's record of all the financial transactions that have taken place; it provides the structure for a company to generate historical financial reporting.

Generally Accepted Accounting Principles (GAAP) – Set of rules and standards for reporting financial accounting information defined by the Financial Accounting Standards Board.

Green field implementation – A new implementation without the need to integrate with existing systems.

Grievance – Employee's formal complaint regarding work-related circumstances.

Human capital – The knowledge, skills, competences, and personality traits an employee possesses to perform labor for the economic value of the firm.

Inventory – A business's goods, materials, and finished and unfinished products that have not been sold yet. Inventory can also include the value of plant and equipment.

IP or intellectual property – Intangible products of the mind that have commercial value such as processes, recipes, copyrighted materials and patents.

Jidoka – The Japanese term for autonomation. This is the ability of an employee to make a decision to stop production, most often because of a defect.

Job population – When used with reference to an employee schedule it refers to the act of filling in open shifts with specific individuals.

Kaizen – The Japanese management philosophy of continuous improvement; examples of continuous improvement include continuous cost reduction, reduced quality problems, and consistent on-time delivery.

Kan ban – Japanese term for card or sign; used to track the flow of materials through the production process.

Key Performance Indicator (kpi) – measurements of performance to evaluate targets set by the firm.

Labor buffer – Extra labor resources waiting for unplanned work to occur.

Labor capacity – The amount of labor available to complete tasks at hand.

Labor costing – The act of allocating labor costs to a product or service.

Labor rate – The standard average hourly rate paid to employees.

Labor variance – Difference between the actual and standard costs of labor.

Lag time – Period of time in-between two related events.

Lead time – Interval of time between initiating a production process and completing it.

Lean (lean manufacturing) – Method for minimizing resources required for production by identifying and eliminating non-value added activities through continuous improvement.

Line pressure – Operating pressure of air or fluid in a hose or pipe on a machine.

Lot size – Amount of units to be manufactured in each operation.

Make to stock – Products are produced to hold as inventory; usually based on sales forecast.

Make vs. buy – The decision by a manufacturer based on a number of factors to determine if they should manufacture their own product component or to purchase it from an outside supplier.

Occupational Safety and Health Administration (OSHA) – An agency of the U.S. Department of Labor that requires employers to maintain safe and healthy working environments for their employees.

Off schedule – Time worked that is not on the employee's regular schedule.

Off the clock – Time actually worked by employees but not recorded and compensated by the company.

Operating expense – The expenses incurred from carrying out day to day activities of a business.

Out of process operations – Activities that can be executed simultaneously with the main process.

Output – Amount produced or work performed by a person, machine, production line or plant.

Over 8 – Greater than a normal 8-hour workday.

Overhead – In manufacturing, all costs related to production except direct labor and materials.

Overtime equalization – A technique that ensures all employees are equally offered opportunities for overtime (they do not have to accept).

Pareto chart – Bar graph showing variances ranked in order of frequency or magnitude.

Pay rule – Pay procedure policies set by the organization; applied to raw worked and leave hours to calculate total hours to be paid.

Payroll inflation – Payroll increase without a corresponding increase in productive output.

Poka yoke – The Japanese term for mistake-proofing; using low-cost procedures to improve quality and prevent defects.

Production cell – Set of machines and operators in close proximity that produce one particular product or product component.

Programmable logic controller (PLC) – Computerized device that captures machine characteristics such as status, quantity produced, cycle time and physical parameters such as temperature and pressure.

Pull system – Production based on actual daily demand rather than forecast.

Return on Investment (ROI) – A measure of the business's profitability; calculated as the net profit after taxes divided by the total assets.

Rounding – The act of adjusting an employee's timestamp to the nearest standard time increment, often a tenth of an hour.

Single Minute Exchange of Dies (SMED) – a technique for reducing the setting up and changeover of equipment.

Six sigma – 5-step process to improve quality and decrease costs by reducing defects; Defined by the following steps: D) Define M) Measure A) Analyze I) Improve C) Control.

Standard in process stock – The quantity of parts always on hand for processing on and between sub-processes.

Standardization of workforce – The ability to document and provide a repeatable process to accomplish a task; important for safety and financial consequences, capturing new and successful ideas, and employee equity and fairness.

Sweetheart scheduling – A supervisor providing preferential treatment in terms of jobs, days or overtime assigned to an individual or group of employees resulting in an unfair allocation of work and pay.

Takt time – Amount of time to produce one component; calculated as work time per units divided by units required by demand.

Throughput – Quantity of production over a period of time.

Time and attendance system – manual or electronic approach to collecting, processing, and storing employee-related data, including times in, out, breaks, and vacation and sick days taken.

Timestamp – Date and time of an event occurrence; in manufacturing, in Workforce Management it usually represents the time an employee begins and ends an activity or shift.

Total quality management – Improve the quality of goods or services by reducing the errors occurring in the manufacturing process.

Unit labor cost – Measure of the cost of the labor needed to produce one unit of some good or service.

Unplanned absenteeism – An employee calling out sick or not showing up for their scheduled shift.

Value stream map – A document describing the flow and duration of activities, materials, and information needed to bring a finished good or service to the end consumer.

Value-added – Those activities that increase the worth of a product from a customer's perspective.

Waste – Any cost or effort applied to product or service that does not add value from a customer's perspective.

Work in process (WIP) – Materials issued to the production floor, but not yet completed into finished products (waiting for further processing).

Work rules – Regulations established concerning the conditions and standards of employee job work, stated within collective bargaining agreements, corporate policy or government regulation.

Workforce Productivity (fiscal definition) – Output divided by cost of labor.

Working sequence – The sequence of operations in a single process which leads an employee to produce quality goods efficiently and in a manner which reduces overburden and minimizes the threat of injury or illness.

Workload generation – Converting production demand into specific labor requirements.